Blog Theory

For Sadie, with love and wonder

Blog Theory

Feedback and Capture
in the Circuits of Drive

JODI DEAN

polity

The right of Jodi Dean to be identified as Author of this Work has been asserted in accordance with the UK Copyright, Designs and Patents Act 1988.

First published in 2010 by Polity Press

Polity Press
65 Bridge Street
Cambridge CB2 1UR, UK

Polity Press
350 Main Street
Malden, MA 02148, USA

ISBN-13: 978-0-7456-4969-6
ISBN-13: 978-0-7456-4970-2(pb)

A catalogue record for this book is available from the British Library.

Typeset in 11 on 13 pt Scala
by Toppan Best-set Premedia Limited
Printed and bound in Great Britain by MPG Books Group Limited, Bodmin, Cornwall

The publisher has used its best endeavours to ensure that the URLs for external websites referred to in this book are correct and active at the time of going to press. However, the publisher has no responsibility for the websites and can make no guarantee that a site will remain live or that the content is or will remain appropriate.

Every effort has been made to trace all copyright holders, but if any have been inadvertently overlooked the publisher will be pleased to include any necessary credits in any subsequent reprint or edition.

For further information on Polity, visit our website: www.politybooks.com

Contents

Acknowledgements

As with so much else at the intersection of new media, politics, and critique, this book was instigated by Geert Lovink. Not only did he push directly for a theoretical pamphlet on blogs and blogging (entitled *Blog Theory* from the outset), but I wrote the second chapter in close email conversation with Geert and in response to his exemplary *Zero Comments*. I am particularly indebted to his insistence on the national and linguistic shapings of the blogipelago as well as to his unparalleled talent in creating the tags and phrases that capture the truths of the media environment.

Exchanges with James Martel helped clarify my thinking about the possibilities for politics that the concept of drive may capture or open up.

Readers of my blog, *I Cite*, have long provided comments, feedback, and new experiences of association (many friendly, some not so much) indispensable for my thinking through of the ways that blogs and social media are coding the kinds of subjects we are becoming. I am particularly indebted to Alain Wittman's thoughtful engagement and continued provocation.

I am grateful to Henk Oosterling and Jos de Mul for the opportunity to present an early version of the discussion of drive and networked media in their seminar in the Faculty of Philosophy at Erasmus University in Rotterdam. I also want to thank Darin Barney from the Department of Art History and Communication Studies at Media@McGill at McGill University for the invitation to present some of my work on whatever blogging as a Visiting Beaverbrook Media Scholar.

Matt Kadane provided valuable suggestions on the history of self-writing. Victoria Lehman and Leah Himmelhoch supplied much needed guidance on reading and writing practices in ancient Rome. Thanks as well to Justin Clemens, Anna Kornbluh, Dominic Pettman, and Ken Wark for their generosity in reading and commenting on various chapters. John Thompson has been supportive and patient since the project's inception.

Sadie and Kian Kenyon-Dean guide me through the turbulence of networked communication and entertainment media, doing their best to keep me up to date. And finally thanks to Paul Passavant for his insight, good humor, and love.

The only conspiracy was a *conspiracy of distraction*. The conspirers, ourselves. If I didn't grasp this law of complicity I should go back to beginning and start again.

Jonathan Lethem, *Chronic City*

1 Blog Settings

1

The challenge of this book is thinking critically about media practices in a setting where they are fast, fun, and ubiquitous. As an avowedly engaged and political approach to thought, critical theory of any sort encounters challenges. Attempting to analyze and intervene in the present, it nonetheless adopts a backward gaze, an idea G.W.F. Hegel figures with the owl of Minerva flying at dawn, Michel Foucault practices through his historical methods of archaeology and genealogy, and Slavoj Žižek conceptualizes with the notion of "retroactive determination." A problem specific to critical media theory is the turbulence of networked communications: that is, the rapidity of innovation, adoption, adaptation, and obsolescence.[1] The object of one's theoretical focus and critical ire quickly changes or even vanishes. The time of theory is over-taken, even taken over, by ever-morphing, interlinking, media.[2]

Since books can easily be surpassed by events, they appear particularly ill chosen as a medium through which to present a critical media theory. A theory that is current, if it is possible at all, seems confined to presentation within the forms and circuits it analyzes. It can be presented in face-to-face conferences, workshops, or meet-ups; it can be posted on discussion lists or blogs. It can be visualized, videoed, shared and distributed, critiqued, amended, sampled, and forwarded. Thought can be made immediate, an element of its moment or, more precisely, of the fantasy that attempts to delimit a moment out of the present's rush to the future and absorption into the past.

A book that makes critical-theoretical claims about blogging thus encounters a double problem of its object and its form of presentation. Each side of the problem entraps theory in its setting. To address its object in a timely fashion, the book has to be new, fresh, up-to-the-minute, fashion-forward, bleeding-edge. It needs to predict or at least hazard a guess as to where things are going, what's going to happen. The book is pushed to adopt, in other words, the entrepreneurial expectations of the venture capitalist, racing to be the first out of the block. This side of the problem highlights one of the specific ways communicative capitalism captures critique and resistance, formatting them as contributions to the circuits in which it thrives.[3] The temporal take-over of theory displaces sustained critical thought, replacing it with the sense that there isn't time for thinking, that there are only emergencies to which one must react, that one can't keep up and might as well not try.

The second side of the problem, the form of theory's presentation, likewise highlights how communicative capitalism fragments thought into ever smaller bits, bits that can be distributed and sampled, even ingested and enjoyed, but that in the glut of multiple, circulating contributions tend to resist recombination into longer, more demanding theories. It's like today we can have and share insights, but these insights must not add up to something like a theory that might aid us in understanding, critically confronting, and politically restructuring the present. Theodor Adorno's criticism of the passion for information in mass culture applies more to contemporary communication and entertainment networks than it did to film and radio, the mass media he has in mind when he writes, "However useful it might be from a practical point of view to have as much information as possible at one's disposal, there still prevails the iron law that the information in question shall never touch the essential, shall never degenerate into thought."[4] As multiple-recombinant ideas and images circulate, stimulate, they distract us from the antagonisms constitutive of contemporary society, inviting us to think that each opinion is equally valid, each option is equally likely, and each click is a significant political intervention. The deluge of images and announcements, enjoining us to react, to feel, to forward them to our friends, erodes critical-theoretical capacities – *aren't they really just opinions anyway? Feelings dressed up in jargon?* Drowning in plurality, we lose the capacity to grasp anything like a system. React and forward, but don't by any means think.

My wager is that critical media theory is possible in book form. The wager is inspired by a time-honored tactic in workers' struggle: the slow-down. As an object whose form installs delays in sampling and syndication and whose content demands postponed gratification, the book mobilizes the gap of mediacy so as to stimulate thought. E-books and articles as well as blog posts on theoretical topics are convenient ways to store and share ideas. But these benefits come at a cost: we pay with attention.[5] It's easy to give into the temptation to keep moving, to follow links, to see what others think about it before one even knows what "it" might be, then to see what else others are thinking about, especially if their posts aren't too long . . . and once we're already a few clicks in, why not go ahead and check our blog stats, update our Facebook profiles, and engage in a few rounds of Mafia Wars or other games helpfully supplied by our favorite social network. It only takes a minute. Or two.

More important, though, is whether the technologies and practices of new media are appropriate objects for critical-theoretical inquiry. Again, my wager is yes. This isn't a risky bet. In recent decades, scholars, artists, and activists working at the interface of communications, media, and cultural studies and social studies of science and technology have developed critical approaches to digital media and their networked environments. Rather than restricted to positivist methods of description and measurement or linear, developmentalist, histories of technical change, this emerging critical media theory anchors its analyses of technologies, users, and practices in an avowedly political assessment of the present.

What that assessment is, or, more specifically, how to theorize the political implications of networked communications and entertainment media, is a matter of passionate disagreement. I take the position that contemporary communications media capture their users in intensive and extensive networks of enjoyment, production, and surveillance. My term for this formation is communicative capitalism. Just as industrial capitalism relied on the exploitation of labor, so does communicative capitalism rely on the exploitation of communication. As Michael Hardt and Antonio Negri argue, "communication is the form of capitalist production in which capital has succeeded in submitting society entirely and globally to its regime, suppressing all alternative paths."[6] A critical theory of communicative capitalism requires occupying (rather than disavowing) the trap in which it enthralls and configures contemporary subjects. I argue that this trap takes the form that modern European philosophy heralded as the form of freedom: reflexivity. Communicative capitalism is that economic-ideological form wherein reflexivity captures creativity and resistance so as to enrich the few as it placates and diverts the many.

2

Communicative capitalism designates the strange convergence of democracy and capitalism in networked communications and entertainment media. On the one hand, networked communications technologies materialize the values heralded as central to democracy. Democratic ideals of access, inclusion, discussion, and participation are realized in and through expansions and intensifications of global telecommunication networks. On the other hand, the speed, simultaneity, and interconnectivity of electronic communications produce massive distortions and concentrations of wealth as communicative exchanges and their technological preconditions become commodified and capitalized. David Harvey explains, "technologies of information creation and capacities to accumulate, store, transfer, analyze, and use massive databases to guide decisions in the global marketplace" have been necessary and essential components of globalized neoliberalism.[7] As the network of networks through which such transactions take place, the internet is the vehicle and terrain for politics and the economy. Changes in communication technologies associated with digitalization, speed (of computer processors as well as connectivity), and memory/storage capacity impact democracy and capitalism, amplifying elements of each as they consolidate the two into a new ideological formation.

The concept of communicative capitalism draws from Žižek's Lacanian-Marxist upgrade of ideology critique. Žižek uses the psychoanalysis of Jacques Lacan to reconfigure the notion of ideology so as to theorize the ways our deepest commitments bind us to practices of domination. Rather than following the commonplace notion that ideology is false consciousness or a term for ideas one doesn't like (the ideas of one's opponents or everybody except the critic), Žižek formats ideology in terms of the beliefs underlying practice. Ideology is what we do, even when we know better (for example, I know that quizzes on Facebook are ingenious ways of collecting information from me and my friends, but I take them anyway). The psychoanalytic notion of fetishism provides a convenient shorthand: "I know, but nevertheless. . . ."

An additional Žižekian concept (one he develops from Claude Lévi-Strauss) important for theorizing communicative capitalism is the decline of symbolic efficiency (aka the collapse of the big Other). If the efficiency of a symbol designates its mobility, its ability to transmit significance not simply from one person to another but from one setting to another, the decline of symbolic efficiency points to an immobility or failure of transmission. Blogs provide a clear example: sometimes it's difficult to tell when a blog or a post is ironic and when it's sincere, when it's funny or when it's serious. Terms and styles of expression that make sense to an "in-group" can shock, insult, or enrage folks who just happen upon a blog. Moreover, the uncertainty, the potential for unexpected meanings, provides its own affective intensity. Images and affects may flow into the gaps left by the declining symbolic. Despite the fact that bloggers generally decry the degeneration of discussion into *ad hominem* attacks and flame wars – nearly always the result of a misunderstanding rather than a disagreement – we secretly enjoy them. Hit rates double, even triple. People become invested in, energized by, the exchange: *how far will she go? She said that!? Oh no she didn't! Pwnd!*[8]

In my first months as a blogger, I had to figure out what my deleting and blocking policy would be. Which comments would I let remain and which would I block? I knew that simply disagreeing with me would not be grounds for deletion – after all, I wanted the blog to be a site for discussion. I decided to delete comments that included explicit racist, sexist, homophobic, and anti-Semitic slurs. Then I got a comment from the GNAA or Gay Nigger Association of America, a group of organized anti-blogging trolls who take their name from a 1992 Danish movie, *Gay-Niggers from Outerspace*. GNAA claims that it promotes neither racism nor homophobia but aims rather to sow disruption on the internet. The comment on my blog was a minor instance of their more extensive disruptive practices (like "crapflooding" a site with a massive amount of text or data with no meaning or relevance: for example, a word, phrase, or group of letters repeated over and over, or producing hoax or shock sites and inserting links or code that redirect viewers to the site).[9]

The concept of the decline of symbolic efficiency is particularly useful for critical media theory as it designates the fundamental uncertainty accompanying the impossibility of totalization: that is, of fully anchoring or pinning down meaning.[10] The contemporary setting of electronically mediated subjectivity is one of infinite doubt, ultimate reflexivization. There's always another option, link, opinion, nuance, or contingency that we haven't taken into account, some particular experience of some other who could be potentially damaged or disenfranchised, a better deal, perhaps even a cure. The very conditions of possibility for adequation (for determining the criteria by which to assess whether a decision or answer is, if not good, then at least adequate) have been foreclosed. *It's just your opinion.* Additionally, as the efficiency of the symbolic declines, images and affective intensities may appear as all the more powerful, relevant, and effective. *A picture is worth a thousand words.*

Žižek uses Lacan to express the point as a suspension of the function of the Master signifier: there is no longer a Master signifier stabilizing meaning, knitting together the chain of signifiers and hindering its tendencies to float off into indeterminacy.[11] The absence of such a Master might suggest a new setting of complete openness and freedom – no authority tells the subject what to do, what to desire, how to structure its choices. Žižek argues, however, that in fact the result of the Master's decline is unbearable, suffocating closure.[12] The online environment Second Life clearly demonstrates this closure: able to do or create anything (there aren't even laws of gravity), the majority of users end up with avatars that are sexier versions of themselves walking around shopping, gambling, fixing up their houses, and trying to meet people ("meet" can be read euphemistically here). It's not only boring – it's stifling as it confronts users with their lack of skills and imagination.

Žižek's account of the decline of symbolic efficiency appears in the context of his critique of risk society theory. Some of the primary themes of this account extend ideas he had previously put to work in early essays on cyberspace and virtual reality. In contrast with a dominant strand of nineties media theory, which treated virtual reality as a new, lawless frontier, Žižek's essays on cyberspace emphasize the virtuality of the symbolic order of meaning and language. The functioning of the Master signifier depends on virtuality. It works not simply as another element in a chain, but as something that is more than itself, something present as potential. Žižek draws an example from Freud: 'the threat of castration has castrating effects.'[13] Cyberspace threatens precisely this fundamental virtuality. The paradox: cyberspace is not virtual enough.

Žižek considers several specific ways virtuality is threatened by computer-mediated interaction. One is the loss of the binding power or performative efficacy of words. Words are no longer "subjectivized" insofar as they fail to induce the subject to stand by them. At any moment, visitors to cyberspace can simply "unhook" themselves. Since exit is an option with nearly no costs, subjects lose the incentive for their word to be their bond. A second threat involves the dissolution of the boundary between fantasy and reality, a dissolution affecting identity and desire. Insofar as digital environments enable the realization of fantasies on the textual screen, they close the

gaps between the subject's symbolic identity and its phantas-
mic background.[14] Instant gratification fills in the lack constitutive of desire. Hypertextual play enables the unstated subtext
of any text to be brought to the fore, thereby eliminating the
textual effects of the unsaid. Put somewhat differently, fantasies that are completely realized cease to be fantasies.[15] A repercussion of this filling-in is a third threat, a threat to meaning.
The gap of signification, the minimal difference that makes
some item or answer significant, that makes it "feel right" or
"the one" dissipates. But instead of eliminating the space of
doubt, the filling-in occasions the loss of the possibility of
feeling convinced, of the sense that an answer can be or is
"right" rather than just another opinion. Žižek asks, "Is not
one of the possible reactions to the excessive filling-in of the
voids in cyberspace therefore *informational anorexia*, the desperate refusal to accept information, in so far as it occludes
the presence of the Real?"[16] It's like the feast of information
results in a more fundamental starvation as one loses the
sense of an underlying Real.

At stake in all three threats – to performativity, desire, and
meaning – is cyberspace's foreclosure of the symbolic (the
elimination of the space of the signifier as it slides into the
Real, which thereby itself loses the capacity to appear as Real).
Žižek treats this foreclosure of the symbolic in the terms of
paranoid psychosis: the Other is both missing and fully, over-
whelmingly present.[17] Yet he doesn't presume the subject's
absorption in the imaginary *jouissance* of a pre-Oedipal primal
oneness. Žižek is careful to note that such an image of friction-
free immersion is "cyberspace capitalism's" own ideological
fantasy, a fantasy of a society without antagonism. What's at
stake, then, is post-Oedipal, an order that doesn't rely on a
Master signifier.[18] In this order, the Real presence of the Other
is lost as the lack in the Other is filled in. The something extra,
the inexpressible mystery or *objet petit a* that makes the Other
Real is subsumed by one who is "*over-present*, bombarding me
with the torrential flow of images and explicit statements of
her (or his) most secret fantasies."[19] Thus, correlative to the
absence of the Real Other are the unbearable intrusions of the
other's *jouissance*.[20]

In sum, the central insight of Žižek's early work on cyberspace involves the change to the symbolic. Žižek argues that the gaps in the symbolic (the gaps that enable access to the Real insofar as the Real cannot be approached directly) are filled in (saturating "the virtual space of symbolic fiction").[21] The result is a situation of non-desire, non-meaning, and the unbearable intrusion of enjoyment. This decline in symbolic efficiency is a fundamental feature of communicative capitalism.

3

The change in the functioning of the symbolic is linked to the reflexivity of complex technological societies. Risk society theory highlights the harms and threats emerging out of increases in complexity. Ulrich Beck, for example, points out that problems ranging from environmental toxicity and climate change to obesity, diabetes, and the threats posed by corporate agriculture are all problems produced by the very technological changes introduced to meet earlier challenges (rapid, efficient transportation, secure and comfortable habitats, adequate food and water, etc.).[22] His point is that scientific knowledge generates new risks and uncertainties. Rather than providing clear answers, it opens up new questions, pushing us to recognize not only that there are unknown unknowns, but that these unknowns can and will have massive, unforeseen effects.[23] Insofar as the effects are unforeseen, they are highly improbable. Insofar as they are networked, these effects are compounded. The consequences of their occurrence, therefore, can be extreme.

During the spring and summer of 2008, mainstream news media expressed anxieties over the imminent start-up of the Large Hadron Collider at CERN (European Organization for Nuclear Research) in Switzerland. A German scientist, Otto Rössler, appealed to the European Court of Human Rights to issue an injunction that would prevent activation of the collider. He argued that the risk to human life was too great. The Large Hadron Collider could create miniature black holes capable of destroying the planet: "My own calculations have shown that it is quite plausible that these little black holes survive and will grow exponentially and eat the planet from the inside."[24] In a 2003 report, CERN had said that black holes were not a conceivable risk, although it addressed in detail the possible creation of "strangelets," hypothetical particles that "could transform the Earth almost instantly into a dead, dense lump."[25] It concluded that this was unlikely. Nonetheless, even with various expert commissions reviewing the scientific evidence, the problem of assessing the relation of risk to probability remained. How is valuation of the existence of the planet and its future generations even possible, particularly in a situation so extreme as to render prediction a kind of high-stakes gambling? After all, a basic premise of quantum mechanics is that most anything could happen, even if its likelihood is very small.

Žižek writes:

> There is a priori no proper measure between the "excess" of scaremongering and the indecisive procrastination of "Don't let's panic, we don't yet have conclusive results.". . . Again, this impenetrability is not simply a matter of "complexity," but of reflexivity: the new opaqueness and impenetrability (the radical uncertainty of the consequences of our actions) is not due to the fact that we are puppets in the hands of some transcendent global Power (Fate, Historical Necessity, the Market); on the contrary, it is due to the fact that "nobody is in charge," that *there is no such power*, no "Other of the Other" pulling the strings – opaqueness is grounded in the very fact that today's society is thoroughly "reflexive". . . .[26]

Human inquiry into the world affects the world. Our relation to the world and to each other is reflexive. Mark C. Taylor explains that "cause and effect are interdependent: the thoughts and actions of agents influence the operation of the system, which, in turn, influences the thoughts and actions of agents."[27] A crucial fact of contemporary life is that more than persisting as an environment we might try to know and understand, the world is also a dynamic effect of our interventions into it – *and we know this*. Hence, we know we impact the world, but we don't know exactly how. Neither do nor can we know with any certainty the ways that our current practices produce some futures while excluding others. We just know that there will be consequences and side-effects that we have not foreseen and that some of these consequences and side-effects will be devastating to some people. A solution to one problem creates countless others.

As Beck points out, scientists' preoccupation with expected effects determines the research process as it channels the lines of inquiry in some directions rather than others. The causality here is recursive: "the *actual* consequences ultimately become more and more incalculable, because the possible effects become more and more estimable and their assessment takes place more and more in the research process and in interaction with its inherent taboo zones, and determine those zones in the course of results."[28] Even our estimations of possible effects have an impact on the world – that we cannot predict. Excesses of information turn into a lack of the information most relevant to the questions at hand.

Contemporary science and technology offer an unbearable, seemingly impossible freedom: the capacity to intervene in the world at the most fundamental levels of matter and energy without being restricted by knowledge of the outcome. Reflection is possible; reflection on the processes and conditions of reflection, on the languages we use and the sciences we have, on the values that lead us in one direction rather than another.[29] Yet this universalized reflexivity cannot determine for us what we ought to do; we are free to do whatever we decide to do, without determination and without cover in some larger, complete, full knowledge, without, in other words, a big Other to ground and secure us. Reflexivity, reflexivity that goes *all the way down*, is thus another name for the decline in symbolic efficiency. The recursive loop is the circuit of the big Other's collapse.

One of Beck's examples of the high-consequence, destabilizing effects of reflexivity is global financial markets. Bubbles, band-wagon effects, and boom-and-bust cycles result from investors' attempts to predict how others will perceive the future even as these very predictions bring a particular future into being. In the words of economist Hyman Minksy (who, having been treated as a fringe thinker by mainstream economists, became better known and more frequently cited in the wake of the economic crises of 2008): "The normal functioning of our economy leads to financial trauma and crises, inflation, currency depreciations, unemployment and poverty in the midst of what could be virtually universal affluence – in short . . . financially complex capitalism is inherently flawed."[30] Beck, though, refers not to Minsky but to financier George Soros.[31] In a number of books, Soros explains his success as a hedge fund manager in terms of what he calls a "theory of reflexivity."[32]

Contra mainstream economics and like Minsky, Soros emphasizes the points of disequilibrium where markets break down. His argument is that markets are not only inefficient but that belief in equilibrium contributes to boom-and-bust cycles insofar as markets are expected to be self-correcting. The reflexivity of market actors with imperfect knowledge (in other words, all market actors) as well as their knowledge that others with imperfect knowledge are nonetheless making investment decisions produces situations of high volatility and low predictability. Again, as Beck makes clear in his discussion of attempts to predict and prevent ill effects of scientific research, reflexivity leads to uncertainty and indeterminacy. One can't be sure what others are doing, and one's guess about what they're doing influences what they do.

Nassim Nicholas Taleb takes Soros's argument a step further: most of our habits of everyday life prevent us from dealing well with uncertainty and indeterminacy. We assume that events in the world around us fall into the shape of a bell-curve (like human height does) and attend rather less to distributions that follow power laws (like citations per author, book sales per author, blog hits, film revenues, wealth of individual capitalists). Hoping and expecting events to fall into a regular pattern, we systematically underestimate the impact of outliers – and this underestimation itself has effects. Like Beck, Taleb emphasizes the ways that the supposition that risks can be measured results in the exclusion of extreme events, precisely the sorts of events – a once-a-century economic crisis or the crash of a very large asteroid into the earth – that can change everything (like Soros, Taleb was able to capitalize on others' failures to allow for extreme events). For all three – Beck, Soros, Taleb – the reflexive structure of communicative capitalism's fast, ubiquitous networks increases the likelihood and impact of high-consequence events. In Taleb's words, "the world in which we live has an increasing number of feedback loops, causing events to be the cause of more events . . . thus generating snowballs and arbitrary and unpredictable planet-wide winner-take-all effects. We live in an environment where information flows too rapidly, accelerating such epidemics."[33] More circuits, more loops, more spoils for the first, strongest, richest, fastest, biggest.[34]

Žižek accepts risk society theorists' emphasis on the uncertainty at the heart of reflexivity, but he argues that they don't go far enough. They fail to consider the effects of reflexivity on contemporary subjectivity, effects that may involve the subject's attachment to new forms of subjection as a way to ease the pressures of the injunctions to succeed, be more, be better, be real, and enjoy. Elsewhere, I explore these effects as they appear in modes of subjectivization constellated around conspiracy thinking and celebrity.[35] In chapter 2, I consider something like the underside or obverse of these modes, the failed subjectivization of whatever being. At stake is the relation between the reflexivity of communicative capitalism and the reflexivity of the subject. Modern European thought construed the autonomy of the subject in terms of its capacity for reflection. Contemporary political theory likewise views democracy reflexively: democratic procedures are forms and vehicles for self-governance; we make the laws we apply to ourselves and these laws make us the people we are. When reflexivity goes all the way down, however, reconfiguring the very form of subjectivity into new sorts of fluid, vulnerable singularities, every aspect and form of which is mutable and contingent, *the endless loop of reflexivity becomes the very form of capture and absorption.* A completely reflexive self is as incompatible with democracy as reflexive self-governance is with fully reflexive subjects.

4

Even as critical thinkers in sociology, psychoanalysis, and economics consider the extremes produced in the circuits of reflexivity, techno-enthusiasts write as if reflexivity were the solution to a wide range of social and political problems. Much of this writing relies on the migration of concepts from cybernetic and complexity theory into commentary on contemporary society, a migration enabled by the rapid growth of networked communications.[36] As computers became tools for everyday life, so did the language of computer networks suggest ways to analyze everyday life.

Among the many popular books documenting, celebrating, and ushering in ubiquitous computing is Steven Johnson's *Emergence: The Connected Lives of Ants, Brains, Cities, and Software*. As the title suggests, Johnson's underlying assumption is that fundamental patterns not only govern but connect seemingly disparate areas of experience: the habits of insects, the neural networks of the human brain, physical interactions among large groups of people, and software code. In all of these, Johnson locates "emergent behavior," patterns and systems that arise and achieve equilibrium through local rules and simple feedback processes. The most striking aspect of emergent behavior is no one commands its patterns to arise or dictates the structures that emerge. Rather, emergent behavior results from "self-organization."

Johnson understands self-organization in terms of sets of opposed concepts: centralized v. decentralized, unified v. distributed, top-down v. bottom-up, and planned v. random. For him, the second term in each pair is both the ideal and the future that we are just beginning to understand. He can valorize these second terms because he presumes equilibrium: that is, he prioritizes homeostasis as the baseline, expected, and default position. Johnson acknowledges that extreme conditions – chaos, clusters, hubs, frenzies – are effects of self-organization, but he thinks that self-organization provides the solution to the instability it creates. The mechanism for this solution is feedback.

Johnson's account of feedback relies on two stories, one about the 1992 media feeding frenzy over President Bill Clinton's alleged affair with Gennifer Flowers and one about the proliferation of "cranks" (trolls) in online discussions. The media brouhaha, he argues, was the result of insufficient negative feedback: "The Flowers episode was an instance of pure positive feedback, unchecked by its opposing force. Each agent's behavior encouraged more like-minded behavior from other agents. There was nothing homeostatic about the process . . ."[37] The tendency of online discussion threads to disintegrate into snark results from the opposite problem. The imbalance between participants and lurkers (those who make points and those who just read them) in threaded discussions enables contrarians to derail conversations. The lack of feedback encourages them to keep up their attacks. With more feedback, though, even online conversations would approach equilibrium.

Johnson writes:

> When you factor in the lurkers, a threaded discussion turns out to be less interactive than a traditional face-to-face lecture, and significantly less so than a conversation around a dinner table, where even the most reticent participants contribute with gestures and facial expressions. Group conversations in the real world have an uncanny aptitude for reaching a certain kind of homeostasis: the conversation moves toward a zone that pleases as much of the group as possible and drowns out voices that offend. A group conversation is a kind of circuit board, with primary inputs coming from the official speakers, and secondary inputs coming from the responses of the audience and other speakers. The primary inputs adjust their signal based on the secondary inputs of group feedback. Human beings . . . are exceptionally talented at assessing the mental states of other people, both through the direct exchanges of spoken language and the more oblique feedback mechanisms of gesture and intonation.[38]

Johnson employs two analogies here. The first obvious one is between human conversations and circuit boards. The second, rather less obvious one is between computer-mediated communication in large, complex, environments and face-to-face interaction, either in a lecture hall or around a dinner table. The blurring between lecture and dinner table enables the analogy with the circuit board and the assumption of homeostasis. Johnson connects primary inputs to official speakers and secondary inputs to an audience.

Do dinner-table conversations typically involve official speakers and an audience? My kids would say yes, but they would do so with a roll of their eyes so as to signal that this isn't ideal and that they would prefer dinner unencumbered by lectures in political theory and psychoanalysis. The more conventional contrast between lecture and dinner-table conversation notes that a lecture is centralized and hierarchical; it relies on the difference between the speaker and her audience. The speaker may be on a stage or at a podium. Her audience faces her, arranged in rows that ensure that people look primarily at her rather than at each other. Conversation over dinner flows among the participants. Ideally, a distinction between speaker and audience never solidifies. A group conversation, then, is *nothing* like a circuit board that relies on primary and secondary inputs. A lecture *might* be like a circuit board, not because of feedback, though, but because the institutional structure of a lecture installs hierarchy, primacy. To make conversation look like a circuit board, then, Johnson has to turn it into a lecture. And this inserts hierarchy, centralization, and top-down organization into a setting that Johnson was attempting to depict as a self-organizing equilibrium.

The analogy with the lecture that enables conversation to be understood in terms of primary and secondary inputs enables Johnson to omit the complexities of actual human interaction and present human beings as "exceptionally talented at assessing the mental states of other people." There is no projection, transference, fantasy, paranoia, or repression; there is no tension or mismatch between what one says and what another hears, between what one says and what one means, or between what one says and why one says it (elements of human interaction that psychoanalysis explores).

At the same time, by treating computer-mediated communication in large, complex environments as if it were no different from face-to-face interaction, Johnson can downplay the ways reflexivity leads to disequilibrium. For him, learning in networked environments means that the extremes fall by the wayside rather than becoming amplified as their effects extend throughout the network. In effect, these extremes become the unknown unknowns already undermining Johnson's reassuring story of homeostasis.

Johnson's omission of complexity and unknownness points to a short-circuit in his account of reflexivity. He writes, "the new software will use the tools of self-organization to build models of our own mental states. . . . They will be mind readers."[39] It appears that his account of emergence depends on a limit that he fails to acknowledge. Reflexivity doesn't go all the way down. If we assume (in an outrageous flight of fancy) that software can read minds (as if minds were made up, as if they were not conflicted, as if there were no unconscious), how would the knowledge we have of the contents of others' minds affect our communication with them? And what about our knowledge that software was reading our minds? How would that impact our interactions and reactions? Would we try to fake out the software, play tricks on it? Would we comply, expecting our every demand to be met such that we become increasingly infantile, unable to tolerate any conflict or discomfort? Johnson neglects these further reflexive twists, the ways that human knowledge has material effects as people bring futures into being on its basis.

The block to reflexivity in Johnson's account arises from the oppositional sets structuring his analysis (not to mention the fantasy-based techno-utopianism obscuring the possibilities of surveillance and control – with mind-reading software, companies could deduct pay from workers day-dreaming on the job; police states could use people's fantasies of destruction as criteria for putting them on terrorist watch lists). Johnson wants to juxtapose "self-organized" to "planned" or "controlled." Thus, he has to avoid considering the networks of communication between people that he treats as self-organized as themselves already implicated in forms of control, an inquiry which would require him to take up the unit that "self" is supposed to designate as well as the ways planning, institutions, and norms are vehicles and conditions for self-organization once one moves from ants to people.

In her discussion of nineties controversies over the self-organizing structure of the internet, Tiziana Terranova suggests that a cybernetic definition of control is "the antithesis of centralized government, because the latter presupposes a complete knowledge of each individual component of the overall system, which is impossible to achieve in these types of structure."[40] One should add that not only is such knowledge impossible to achieve in any political structure, but also that the invocation of such control as a critique of centralized planning aims at a straw man: theories and practices of centralized government have never been based on complete knowledge of each individual component – political power as such is exercised as potential: that is, as a promise, expectation, or threat.

Terranova notes that the "biological turn" that emphasizes the life-like qualities of complex systems generally rejects governmentality as unsuited to the turbulent terrain of dynamic networks and deregulated markets.[41] This rejection, however, overlooks the changes in governmentality that subjected the state to the market. As Foucault explores in his lectures on neoliberalism, insofar as neoliberalism emphasizes the market as a site of competition rather than exchange, it demands that the state combat anti-competitive mechanisms and work to spread opportunities for competition. The state must be ever vigilant in these efforts as well as vigilant about its own efficiency. Moreover, such vigilance is exercised not just with regard to government, as its operations and resources are privatized. Rather, neoliberalism entails a governmentality of "active, multiple, vigilant, and omnipresent" intervention in society, an intervention exercised through and by multiple networks traversing micro and macro domains.[42]

Johnson's account of emergence presupposes the cybernetic definition of control that Terranova invokes. With such a presupposition, Johnson cannot acknowledge reflexivity's operation as a dynamic of control: that is, the ways that the extremes produced by the circulation of information themselves have effects on those of us captured in communicative capitalism.

5

Fred Turner's history of cyberculture puts in perspective both Johnson's infatuation with emergence and the sets of oppositional categories supporting it. Turner focuses on the "New Communalists," the 1960s Bay Area counterculture movement. Crucial to Turner's discussion is the transformation of the computer from a tool of control, hierarchy, and dehumanization to computing as the technology of collaboration, flexibility, and utopian social change. To explain how this happened, Turner distinguishes between the New Communalists and the New Left. Whereas the New Left emphasized political struggle – that is, organizing to try to bring about a better world (registering voters, forming parties, staging demonstrations) – for the New Communalists, "political activism was at best beside the point and at worst part of the problem."[43] The New Communalists rejected left notions of conflict, imagining instead a world of networks wherein the most fundamental struggles were those of the individual for the information he (and it was nearly always he) needed for personal freedom and transformation.

The central figure in Turner's story is Stewart Brand, founder of the *Whole Earth Catalog* in 1968 and (with computer entrepreneur Larry Brilliant) the influential teleconferencing system the WELL (Whole Earth 'Lectronic Link) in 1985. As a Stanford undergraduate at the end of the fifties, Brand shared the concern of many coming of age during the Cold War – fear of annihilation, either by nuclear war or by the stifling conformity of mass society. Over the next decades, he explored positive alternatives, including psychedelic drugs, performance art, communal living, the teachings of Buckminster Fuller, personal computing, and entrepreneurialism.

Brand's skills as a networker, as well as his success in combining metaphors of individual consciousness, energy, and

self-organizing systems, contributed to the vision of collaborative, harmonious information networks that helped usher in
the internet. Turner uses the *Whole Earth Catalog* as an
example. Including consumer items and information resources
as seemingly incongruous as mystical fiction and geodesic
domes, the catalog suggested a vision of life that combined
nomadic tribes and high-tech electronics in a frontier fantasy
of do-it-yourself American freedom. A libertarian fantasy, this
ideal of freedom disavowed its position within a capitalist
economy and concealed its dependence on other people,
industries, and institutions. The right technology would
engender total individual self-reliance, in effect making the
Kantian dream of autonomy a material reality.

Brand's New Communalist ideal presented itself as a
counter to the militarist, bureaucratic, corporate establishment. Turner details how the ideal actually embraced the most
fundamental components of what it ostensibly rejected,
namely, "the technocentric optimism, the information theories, and the collaborative work style of the research world."[44]
The post-war era's enormous government-funded research
projects, although housed in bureaucracies, actually employed
interdisciplinary teams working collaboratively across a variety
of fields and agencies. This collaborative ethos should not be
surprising: the development of large-scale weapons systems
required both a language capable of combining humans and
machines, cybernetics, and tools for handling knowledge,
computers. In taking over systems theory and the collaborative
practices of military research, then, the New Communalists
assumed as their own the basic practices and suppositions of
their opponent.

Three aspects of the New Communalist adoption of the
military-research model of information and technology should
be kept in mind. The first is its core faith: technology will save
the world.[45] Just as military planners thought that computers,
surveillance, information, and speed would defeat the enemy
in the future, so did the New Communalists follow the credo
that the proper tools make anything possible; the computer
thus appears as the universal tool making *everything* possible.
Second, as they adopt the faith (information, technology,

systems) while denying its institutions (military, bureaucracy, corporation), the New Communalists "reintroduced many of the core principles of research culture into American society – but this time, as the intellectual foundations of a *counter*culture."[46] What had been a marker and instrument of oppression reversed into its opposite. Collaboration, flexibility, technological skill, and the capacity to generate and share information would produce not imperial control but new, freer, and more fulfilled modes of being. Third, the New Communalist adoption of cybernetics and reproduction of its logics as liberating contributed to political, economic, and cultural change: the rise of neoliberalism. By the end of the eighties, the new "digerati" (some of whom had participated in conferences organized by Brand) could successfully apply the New Communalist formula of conjoining "the cultural legitimacy of the counterculture to the technological and economic legitimacy of the computer industry."[47] In 1987, Brand co-founded the Global Business Network, a consulting firm that encouraged collaborative research and organizational practice. Its clients included "the same corporate and military institutions that the New Communalists and the New Left had condemned."[48]

Turner's history of cyberculture provides the broader setting in which Johnson's oppositional sets – centralized v. decentralized, unified v. distributed, top-down v. bottom-up, and planned v. random – may have at one time made sense. The New Communalists understood their project as countercultural, a rejection of the establishment world that threatened them with absorption in a technocratic project not of their own making. Because they opposed the military–industrial complex, state centralism, and hierarchical corporate structures, they presented their efforts toward individual empowerment, information sharing, and networked collaboration as necessarily counter to these forms of control. In this way, they missed how the military, state, corporation, and university were already functioning in distributed, decentralized networks. Thus, they failed to acknowledge how their ostensibly countercultural practices themselves served as the conduits for spreading the communication and control mechanisms of the technocratic research world not just throughout US society but, via the internet, throughout most of the world. The very mechanisms that were supposed to enable local practices, freedom from commercial, corporate expectations, and opportunities to cultivate a variety of ways of being produced the networks through which communicative capitalism ensnares speech and action.

Christopher Kelty's notion of "recursive publics" should also be understood in light of the reversal of the terms and practices of the state and corporation into the oppositional categories of the counterculture and back into those of the neoliberal state. Kelty introduces "recursive publics" in his ethnography of "Free Software." For him, Free Software is a movement that extends out from technical software projects to encompass "a considerable reorientation of knowledge and power in contemporary society – a reorientation of power with respect to the creation, dissemination, and authorization of knowledge in the era of the Internet."[49] More than the initial practices of the programmers whose work built the internet, more than the efforts of hackers and geeks to liberate proprietary source code, and more than the legal struggles around copyright and fair use, Free Software, Kelty argues, is about equality, fairness, and justice.

This interpretation of Free Software rests on the articulation of values of individual empowerment, collaboration, and information sharing ushered in by Brand and his New Communalists. Kelty repeatedly points out that Free Software is not opposed to capitalism. He gestures (with apparent enthusiasm and approval) to the libertarian impulses of the Brand-affiliated technophiles grouped around *Wired* in the early nineties, Esther Dyson, Howard Rheingold, and John Perry Barlow. He cites uncritically a "famous bit of Internet-governance folklore": "We reject kings, presidents, and voting. We believe in rough consensus and running code."[50] The "reorientation of knowledge and power" that Kelty describes is the reorientation at the basis of communicative capitalism, the reorientation behind the last thirty years of neoliberal excess and its increases in inequality and immiseration that have paraded around as expansions in information, flexibility, participation, and responsiveness. Presuming that the work of programmers is analogous to politics, Kelty routes around conflict, as if working code were the solution to any problem rather than a particular set of problems. Likewise proceeding as if government and market were the same, Kelty absorbs concerns with public goods and the well-being of the many into private interests, an absorption that benefits the very, very rich and eviscerates states' abilities to pay for social security as generally understood. He omits the fact that the reorientation of knowledge and power he describes has ushered in the winner-take-almost-all markets of extreme neoliberalism. Geeks may be about equality, fairness, and justice among each other (or, as is more likely, they may be about competition and glory, killer apps and venture capital). How they feel isn't the point, particularly when these feelings displace attention from communicative capitalism's installation of heretofore unseen extremes of inequality because the reflexivity of complex networks leads to power law distributions.[51] Even if geeks are "about" justice and equality, the consequence of the widespread adoption and extension of their work is the most extreme economic inequality the world has ever known.

Kelty writes:

> The proliferation of hybrid commercial–academic forms in an era of modifiability and reusability, among the debris of standards, standards processes, and new experiments in intellectual property, results in a playing field with a thousand different games, all of which revolve around renewed experimentation with coordination, collaboration, adaptability, design, evolution, gaming, playing, worlds, and worlding. These games are indicative of the triumph of the American love of entrepreneurialism and experimentalism; they relinquish the ideals of planning and hierarchy almost absolutely in favor of a kind of embedded, technically and legally complex anarchism. It is here that the idea of a public reemerges: the ambivalence between relinquishing control absolutely and absolute distrust of government by the few.[52]

Like Johnson and like the New Communalists, Kelty relies on an opposition between planning and experimentation and top-down v. bottom-up. At the same time as he disavows the ways the "thousand different games" result in an absolute disparity between the one who wins and the many who lose (*hey, they all got to play, right?*), he treats law as just another element of a complex market rather than a means by which the people govern themselves. In an age where lawyers employed by the administration of George W. Bush use legal complexities to argue for the legality of torture and economists with the Barack Obama administration use legal complexities to enable massive redistributions of public funds to private banks, "legally complex anarchism" skirts way too close to illegality: that is, to a suspension of law in the celebration of its gaps and exceptions.

More objectionable, though, is Kelty's treatment of the games of entrepreneurs as the same as public supervision of the activities of elected representatives, even when, especially when, their activities are not connected with government-sponsored public projects. In the scenario Kelty describes, the builders of communication networks are governing the rest of us (proceeding without our consent and generally beneath our awareness). They are a technocratic elite unburdened by constraints of representation or oversight. The programmers don't just build software; they act for the people – although this acting is itself formatted in terms of communicative capitalism's merging of markets and governance.

What makes geek jobs (whether voluntary, freelance, or corporate) the activities of a *demos*? To whom are the geeks accountable? Who oversees them? Who determines whether what they've made is good, right, or legitimate? What if non-geeks want to participate? Or what if they understand their creative, productive, affective work as the proper field of political determination? Kelty claims that "recursive publics" (the only example of which is Free Software) are democratic checks on constituted power.[53] They may well be checks, but they are checks without authorization or legitimacy, checks motivated by the "entrepreneurial and experimental" interests of those who work in telecommunications networks. There is nothing "democratic" about them.

I can approach this point from another direction. Jürgen Habermas initially developed the notion of the public sphere as a category of bourgeois society. The public sphere was a form for subjecting absolutism to the political authority of the bourgeoisie. Publicity functioned as a principle of control that remade the political in its own terms, even as this very remaking "renounce[d] the form of claim to rule."[54] Paradoxically, publicity as an ideal emerged as a counter-power via associations that were secret and exclusive: the ideals of publicity initially circulated in secret societies like Freemasonry.

Reinhart Koselleck, whose *Critique and Crisis* preceded and influenced Habermas's *Structural Transformation of the Public Sphere*, views these secret societies as crucial to publicity's remaking of the political. They were the means through which the aura of power was transferred from the mysteries of the monarch to the arcana of the lodges. These institutions were secret inner spaces within the absolutist state, spaces that were separated from the political by the very mysteries whose protections enabled the lodges to serve indirectly as a counter to the state. Ritualized spaces of non-familial, non-market relations, the lodges provided forms of association and experiences of connection beyond those established by absolutism. They established their own standards and habits of judgment. Koselleck emphasizes that this new form of social pressure, this new moral force that had to forgo direct coercion, "was always simultaneously an act of passing more judgment on the State."[55] Because the lodges distinguished themselves from the state, because they positioned themselves as avowedly moral and non-political, they set themselves not simply apart from politics, but above it, in a new domain they were ushering into being. Refusing to acknowledge their actions as political, they subjected the state instead to their moralizing gaze.[56] They were political actors who denied their politics.

Kelty's geeks function analogously to Koselleck's lodges. Both are groups that treat their own norms and practices as those to which society as a whole is or should be subjected even as they deny their political investments. Kelty presents "geeks" as outside government and industry even as they work within them, as outside of politics even as they endeavor to serve and enhance capitalism. He identifies their work with a moral idea of order associated both with The Public (capitalization in original) and with specific norms of "availability, reusability, and modifiability."[57] These norms thereby emerge as seemingly neutral and unquestionably appropriate standards for societal judgment. Moreover, as in Habermas's initial account of the bourgeois public sphere, which disappears at the moments of its materialization in mass communication as the critical role of the idealized public is displaced by the consumerist orientation of the public, so in Kelty's does the "recursive public" recede in the wake of the mass uptake of computer-mediated communication. Geek norms emerge, claim neutrality and appropriateness, and then retreat, leaving in their wake a pro-capitalist, entrepreneurial, and individualistic discourse of evaluation well suited for the extension and amplification of neoliberal governmentality. Differently put, the "recursive public" appears only retroactively, in Kelty's idealization of the libertarian technical impulse that celebrates exercises in expanding and intensifying privately owned platforms and applications as democracy.

6

Turner's New Communalists and Kelty's Free Software function as "displaced mediators." I offer the term "displaced mediator" as an upgrade of the notion of the "vanishing mediator," introduced by Fredric Jameson and elaborated further by Žižek. For Jameson and Žižek, the vanishing mediator is a transitional figure – of an institution, practice, idea – that accounts for a fundamental change. The vanishing mediator triggers a process of change even as change quickly overtakes it. Jameson refers to the Protestant work ethic as the vanishing mediator between feudalism and capitalism and to the Jacobins as the vanishing mediator between the political structures of absolutism and bourgeois rule. Each serves as a "catalytic agent which permits an exchange of energies between two otherwise mutually exclusive terms."[58] Žižek uses the East European transition to capitalism to make the same point. During the months of socialist upheaval, a chaotic array of punks, artists, and activists flourished in a heady mix of democratic activity. Once the new regime established itself, once it adopted the language of democracy as its own, these same movements either vanished or began to stand for their opposite, "protocommunists."[59] Again, the logic is one wherein what was previously an external presupposition (an opposing force, say) comes to be posited as an inherent moment, thereby obliterating the prior open and antagonistic condition.

Given that the mediators Jameson and Žižek describe don't vanish but remain present in a different form, whether ideally, oppositionally, or as practices and aspirations the pressure of which we continue to feel, I think of them as displaced mediators. After all, there are still Protestants. There are still work ethics. The Jacobins' ideals of equality, freedom, and solidarity continue to exert a kind of signifying stress (a term from Eric Santner) on our failures to have realized them. And East European activists and artists continue to struggle against nationalism, capitalism, and democracy as the political form both have taken. To refer to these mediators as "vanishing," then, suggests a victory in situations in which contestation continues. Rather than participating in this disappearance, the term "displaced mediator" designates mediators whose functions have been displaced from what appears (retroactively) as their previous role.

The New Communalists, then, are displaced mediators in the sense that they turned the practices and suppositions of the military–corporate research complex into the ideals and suppositions of a counterculture. The "recursive public" of Free Software claims to incorporate and extend ideals of flexibility, changeability, and reprogrammability. Yet the networks of communicative capitalism at the basis of Free Software instead produce inequality, insecurity, and subjection to the conditions and demands of a recalcitrant finance sector. What proferred itself as a vehicle for bringing in something new, something better, becomes the mechanism for further embedding and extending the old, now strengthened by the rhetoric of its own over-coming.

The term "displaced mediator" indexes displacement in multiple registers. Here are three. First, along with the political-economic change effected though the mediators as human groups, media themselves may be displaced by the events and

developments they enable. For example, mainframe computers stimulated cooperative time-sharing practices that valo-
rized the ideals of collaboration and adaptation necessary for
advances in personal and networked computing. Such super-
computers are still functioning, but their place in the computing imaginary has shifted. Although they are current, they
seem like relics.

Second, emphases on specific media and technologies risk
displacing attention from their settings. Here, media stand in
for (sometimes occluding) larger, more systemic political and
economic changes. Widespread uptake in participation on a
commercial social network like Facebook or MySpace may
displace (as well as supplement or enhance) other practices
and activities – pick-up basketball or going door to door to
collect signatures for a campaign, say – practices and activities
that then come to be viewed themselves in media terms. So,
texting enables kids to arrange basketball games or online
petitions make signature gathering faster and easier. What's
displaced from view are the pleasures and benefits accompanying the prior mode of being. More fundamentally, enthusiasm
over new gadgets and apps, communicative sites and practices
– like Twitter, Facebook, and blogging – displaces critical
attention from their setting in communicative capitalism.

Third, the history of networked communications is filled
with displaced mediators: semaphores, telegraphs, CB radios,
records, eight-track tape, videotape, landlines, pagers, BBSs,
usenet, alternet, homepages, portal sites – not to mention film,
television, mobile phones, and the internet. Over a decade ago,
Bruce Sterling put together a web-based project to archive
"dead" and obsolete media.[60] To consider such media as displaced is to consider them in and as settings, in and as imbri-
cated in political, economic, and affective circuits. The concept
of displaced media, then, is a critical one. Media appear as
displaced from the perspective of a backward look. Their displacement is retroactively determined in the context of an
attempt to pull an explanation out of the multiplicity and contingency of technological change. Thus, a benefit of "displaced
media" is that it yields "newness" in advance. Rather than
linking critical media theory to its currency – has it kept up

and incorporated the latest techno-trends? – the idea of displaced media embeds the instability and volatility of media practices into the analysis.

7

Blogging emerges as a practice in communicative capitalism. Not only are blogs "natively digital," but the practices of posting, linking, commenting, reacting, measuring, and circulating make mediated reflexivity available to virtually anyone who wants to bother. Even if a blog post is more than a reaction, more than a commentary on something else, its invitation to read, comment, and share installs it in communicative capitalism's flows of information and entertainment. Blogging's settings, then, include the decline of symbolic effi-ciency, the recursive loops of universalized reflexivity, the extreme inequalities that reflexive networks produce, and the operation of displaced mediators at points of critical transition. Its default mode is captured.

Rather than treating blogs as cutting-edge forms of participatory journalism or new experiments in an already mundane exhibitionism, I proceed from the assumption that they are displaced mediators. Even if they're not dead yet, their role in inciting practices of online disclosure, discussion, and surveillance has both already been displaced by other Web 2.0 platforms such as social networks and video-sharing and itself displaced attention from the profound inequalities produced and amplified by global financial and entertainment networks. Differently put, as displaced mediators, blogs access key features of communicative capitalism: the intensification of mediality in reflexive networks (communicating about communicating), the emergence of "whatever beings" (beings who belong but not to anything in particular), and the circulation of affect (as networks generate and amplify spectacular effects). This access not only draws out the challenges to political organization under current conditions but also highlights the imperative for actually undertaking such organizing rather than presuming it will simply emerge: the very practices of media we enjoy, the practices that connect us to others and ostensibly end our alienation, appropriate and reassemble our longings into new forms of exploitation and control.

Key to the argument of this book is the claim that Lacan's version of the psychoanalytic concept of drive expresses the reflexive structure of complex networks. For Lacan, the drive is "beyond the instinct to return to the state of equilibrium."[61] Its very excess renders it akin to a "will to create from zero, a will to begin again."[62] Lacan's description here evokes the self-organized criticality of complex networks. Accelerations and repetitions throughout their circuits gain in momentum and intensity – feeding frenzies, vicious circles, bubbles – until they result in extreme or catastrophic ruptures, zero points from which something new begins.

The repercussion of this claim is that what idealists from the Enlightenment, through critical and democratic theory, to contemporary techno-utopians theorize as the very form of freedom is actually a mechanism for the generation of extreme inequality and capture. Just as enthusiasts for emergence, anarchy, and Free Software presume in advance the progressive radicality of being beyond law, governance, and the state, so have some psychoanalytically inspired theorists too quickly presumed that liberation can be found beyond desire and the law. I argue that beyond the law are the reflexive circuits of drive. Communicative capitalism thrives not because of unceasing or insatiable desires but in and as the repetitive intensity of drive.

Lacan conceives drive as necessarily death drive (rather than agreeing with Freud's view of eros as also a drive). This death drive ruptures equilibrium. Such an explicit negativity can interrupt and counter the slide from networked computers into networks as biological swarms and patterns. Although typically associated in the theoretical literature with biopolitics or biopower, the elision from biological metaphor to networked communication appears throughout popular techno-utopianism, particularly that techno-utopianism blending neoliberalism (entrepreneurialism, free markets, anti-regulation) and the internet. I see this rather unexpected union of computers and *bios* as symptomatic of a new essentialism:

network logics are dictates of nature, a new form of natural law that immanently and necessarily yields the unity and convergence of all things to the extent that they are allowed to flow freely. Just like the spread of lily-pads in a pond, the analogy goes, so will blogs and other innovations emerge and die, flourish and struggle. Absorbed in a supposition of immanent reconciliation, extremes of distribution become natural facts, outgrowths of abundant potential. The notion of drive counters this immanent naturalism by highlighting the inhuman at the heart of the human, the cut or break with the flow of life, the peculiar and uncanny human propensity to become stuck on minor activities and minimal differences. Conceived in terms of drive, networked communications circulate less as potentials for freedom than as the affective intensities produced through and amplifying our capture.

My discussion of drive draws heavily from Žižek, but there is a difference. Žižek emphasizes that the "stuckness" of drive (what I've been treating as capture) is the intrusion of a radical break or imbalance: "drive is quite literally *the very 'drive' to break the All of continuity in which we are embedded*, to introduce a radical imbalance into it."[63] My argument is that communicative capitalism is a formation that relies on this imbalance, on the repeated suspension of narratives, patterns, identities, norms, etc. Under conditions of the decline of symbolic efficiency, drive is not an act. It does not break out of a set of given expectations because such sets no longer persist as coherent enchainments of meaning. On the contrary, the circulation of drive is functional for the prevention of such enchainments, enchainments that might well enable radical political opposition. The contemporary challenge, then, is producing the conditions of possibility for breaking out of or redirecting the loop of drive.

One of the stranger aspects of communicative capitalism is new media activists' faith in the ideologies of networks and publicity. Activists continue to emphasize the democratic potential of the internet, even in the face of the increases in economic inequality and consolidation of neoliberal capitalism in and through globally networked communication. They continue to embrace the notion of a value added in networks as if through a magical process of accrual, a magic of networks that would transform politics just as it transformed the economy into something else. The only reason for accepting this magical thinking is if one thinks that there is no politics other than the market, if one assumes, in other words, that the market has not only displaced but taken the place of the political. Such a lack or absence of the political is the hole around which networked communications circulate. Or, more precisely, this loss of a capacity to think the political circulates as drive.

To return back to where I started, my wager is for critical media theory (in book form). And the wager is that critical media theory is possible when it occupies the trap of its emergence, not when it offers happy solutions (the happiness of which would necessarily belie the severity of the problems it diagnoses) and not when it presumes that an analysis of entrapment or capture is the same thing as escape (which would presuppose that the trap was a pseudo trap of words all along). In the reflexive networks of communicative capitalism, a media theory that is critical has to foreswear the affective enterprise of contributing the feeling-impulses of hope and reassurance and offer thinking instead.

2   The Death of Blogging

1

A sure sign of the triumph of a practice or idea is the declaration of its death. Early in the summer of 2007, the bell tolled for blogging – despite the fact that the number of blogs had exceeded seventy million and was continuing to rise. Throughout the ostensibly dead blogosphere, word spread rapidly that blogs had been killed by boredom, success, and even newer media (a weird contradiction whereby the content of the news was belied by the form of its blogged announcement).

For some the newness had worn off. Having blogged, they were ready for something else. Some blog writers tired of the demands of the format for regular updates; "they said what they had to say and moved on."[1] Some blog readers lost interest in the daily activities of so-called "A-listers." Familiar with the voices and perspectives of widely popular long-term bloggers, they began turning their attention elsewhere, to making videos for YouTube or lolcats for "I Can Has Cheezburger." Others lamented the repetitiveness of blog debates. After a few months of reading a given blog or frequenting a set of sites in the blogipelago,[2] predicting the range of responses to any given post or comment was easy. In the words of a blogger quoted in an Australian newspaper, "The same old people saying the same old things. Boring. Boring. Boring."[3] Wasn't the increasing number of abandoned blogs, of ghost blogs with one or two posts left behind by those who tried blogging and then realized they had better ways to spend their time, clear evidence that blogging was dying as a practice?

No. Accompanying the apparently rising rates of blog death was a phenomenon indicative of blogging's vitality even as it was a culpable suspect in the death of blogging – the rise of corporate blogs. Well before the summer of 2007, blogs seemed to have reached a saturation point. Corporations had begun to monitor, intervene in, and attempt to produce conversations. As the Brand Republic website urged, "By getting involved in user-generated content, you can get more people involved in your brand than they have ever been before, increase their loyalty, even make them your brand advocates. And you can find out exactly what they think about your product."[4] Blogs provided access to information about customers' likes and dislikes, trends and buzz previously available only in the survey snapshots of pollsters. By starting their own blogs, hiring bloggers, and participating in discussions related to their products, companies could market in another mode. They could tap niches and build brand awareness through more direct interactions with potential customers – even as they faced the problem of attracting readers to their blogs, of promoting their promotions, or advertising their advertising.[5] By 2009, 70 percent of bloggers said they blogged about brands.[6]

With brand attachment as a primary goal, corporate blogging came up against a key element of blogging: the conceit of authenticity. How could a blog ostensibly written by a logo or branded media image or even an actual person paid to blog by the company offer anything but spin? What would be the attraction of a blog that was all advertising? Why would anyone visit that? In 2006, for example, bloggers outed McDonald's for foisting a fake blog on unsuspecting viewers in ads for the Super Bowl.[7] Even worse were the computer-generated spamblogs or splogs.[8] Spamblogs scrape and grab content from anywhere on the internet and dump it on a blog that has been automatically generated. This content then shows up higher in search-engine results since it appears that more people are linking to it. When one searches the content and follows the link, one ends up at site with a bunch of ads and thus contributes to the site-owner's ad revenue. In December 2006, splogs were being created at the rate of about eleven thousand a day.[9]

Combined with the generally recognized banality of most blogs, the proliferation of blog trash suggested a technology and a practice that had exceeded its use-by date.

As blogging apparently suffocated under the excesses of its own success, new applications appeared to take its place or, better, join it in an ever-intensifying expansion of media applications and practices. Some commentators viewed these new applications as more nails in blogging's coffin. Blogging was good while it lasted, but it was no longer fresh. It wasn't politically bold or culturally innovative, but rather the way one's aunt displayed her cat photos. New applications seemed to be changing the conditions of possibility for blogging. With the addition of podcasting, photoblogging, and videoblogging, the platform had been stretched as far as it could go.

The most frequently invoked blog killers were large social networking sites like Facebook and MySpace, but microblogging practices like Twitter (a merging of SMS – Short Message Service or texting – and the internet created in 2006) were not far behind. Facebook and MySpace reconfigure the link, post, comment, and archive structure associated with blogs. Rather than oriented around daily or even weekly posts on a regular set of themes or from a particular perspective, these large social network sites rely on brief, frequent updates to user profiles, lots of photos, and ever-growing lists of friends. Blog updates can be syndicated into one's profile and links can be shared with one's friends, but unlike blogs' reliance on the persona of the blogger, social network sites prioritize connections to others – whoever and whatever the others might be (bands, groups, and products are all available as potential "friends" on MySpace). Contacts matter more than information, angle, or opinion. Social network sites let one see one's connections, the others who are more than an audience of readers, the colleagues and family members and friends of friends that constitute the communities that traverse specific locations. Able quickly and easily to update one's "friends" on what one is doing, one doesn't have to spend a great deal of time involved with specific, individual, people. It's like friendship lite or friendship without friendship (in other words, it's in the overall series of objects or practices deprived of their harmful features that Slavoj Žižek associates with contemporary culture: beer without alcohol, sugar-free candy, coffee without caffeine, etc.). Even better: social network sites let us see ourselves being seen. Instead of writing for strangers, a characteristic of blogs insofar as they are available to search engines, social network sites privilege sharing with friends, with a circuit of others that one has explicitly "friended."

Like Facebook and MySpace, Twitter also relies on social networks and short entries. Mobile users text entries – "tweets" – of 140 characters or fewer as they go about their days, updating their "followers" on where they are, what they are doing, and what they think or feel at any given moment. It's like blogging stripped to its most banal, repetitive, and nonetheless connective and intimate features. A benefit over blogs is brevity – one can keep up without having to spend much time doing it – and mobility – one can post and receive updates via mobile phone so one can always be connected.

More significant is the performance of authenticity enabled by Twitter – along with Facebook's newsfeed and the mood updates on MySpace: the short glimpses into someone's life as it is being lived *seem real*.[10] They seem real in part because they are only glimpses, fragments, and indications rather than fully formed and composed reflections and in part because we witness them being seen by others.

Obscuring the larger setting of communicative capitalism, the declaration that blogs are dead hinders our thinking about contemporary media practices and their additive, supplementary, interlinking dimensions. Social network sites and Twitter don't replace blogs; they traverse, extend, and include them. According to the 2009 State of the Blogosphere report, 73 percent of bloggers v. 14 percent of the general population use Twitter – the percentage use among professional bloggers is even higher; all bloggers say their number one use of Twitter is promoting their blogs.[11] Ignoring the intermediation of contemporary communicative practices, the proclamation that blogs are dead repeats the criticisms of blogging that accompanied its emergence: blogging is parasitic, narcissistic, pointless. Since these criticisms neither prevented the rapid uptake of blogging nor actually cohere insofar as the accusations of parasitism and narcissism presume a point to blogging even as they wrongly reduce blogs to either commentaries on other media or accounts of people's everyday experiences, they are better understood as descriptions. Blogging *is* parasitic, narcissistic, and pointless – *and this is why internet users all over the world blog in ever-increasing numbers.*

The evidence offered for the death of blogs points to blogging's life even as it indexes ongoing turbulence – innovation and obsolescence – in media practices. As one blogger noted,

> hardly a day goes by without some intellectual or journalist or other member of the only-our-opinion-counts brigade writing something about how awful, stupid, passé, dumb, rude, uninteresting or otherwise unacceptable blogs are. My unwanted advice to such writers is that if blogs really are as uncaptivating as you keep saying, and are as rapidly on their way to oblivion as you keep breathlessly announcing, then stop writing about them.[12]

Critical media theory easily risks the same mistake, proceeding as if networked media practices necessarily contain or accompany a guerilla politics of minoritarian disruption ("hacktivism") rather than emerge and persist as components of a vast commercial entertainment culture that has found a way to get the users to make the products they enjoy and even pay to do it.

Just as the newness wore off for some English-language early adopters, millions more across the globe were taking up blogging.[13] Some of the most significant growth is in Asia: over 61 percent of Chinese internet users have created blogs (compared to 18 percent in the UK, 21 percent in the US, and 8 percent in Germany) and over 80 percent of internet users in China, South Korea, and Malaysia have read blogs.[14] In 2006 there were more blog posts per hour in Japanese than there were in English.[15] That there was no longer an "A-list" of elite bloggers (nearly always centered in and on the US) didn't mean blogging was dead – it meant that more people were blogging, that there were more blogs to read, and that the blogipelago was growing, expanding, diversifying. It meant, in other words, that blogging had become an active component of contemporary media's circuits.

To accentuate the diversity among blogs, the way that bloggers do not constitute some kind of natural group, understand themselves as a collective, or interact in a common space, not least because of differences in language, culture, location, and interest, I favor the term "blogipelago" over the more common "blogosphere." The term "sphere" suggests a space accessible to any and all. It implies a kind of conversational unity, as if bloggers addressed the same topics and participated in one giant discussion. The term "blogosphere" tricks us into thinking community when we should be asking about the kinds of links, networks, flows, and solidarities that blogs hinder and encourage. "Blogipelago," like archipelago, reminds us of separateness, disconnection, and the immense effort it can take to move from one island or network to another. It incites us to attend to the variety of uses, engagements, performances, and intensities blogging contributes and circulates.

Corporate uptake of blogging, while a nuisance to long-time bloggers, is a market version of the expansion and diversification of blogs. While apparent in companies' enthusiasm for identifying ever more specific niche tastes and markets, the drive to monetize work and content seemingly offered free of charge accelerates blogging's centripetal momentum. Far from inaugurating a new creative, post-monetary commons, media practices like blogging and social networks ease the paths of neoliberal capitalism. Why should employers pay for work that we happily do for free?

Blogging lives. Rather than "the lingering remainders of a cultish enthusiasm for self-expression that is rapidly wearing off," the new technological forms and practices emerging around and from blogging indicate the spread and morphing of drives to connect and express.[16] My concern here is to theorize critically the widespread uptake of blogging as a practice that emerges in a rapidly changing communications environment. Blogging is a way to access the current conjuncture of media, subjectivity, and politics, a conjuncture that I argue is best understood via the reflexive circuit of drive.

2

Blogging has been associated with murder and death ever since the mainstream media starting noticing it (around 2002). Just like video killed the radio star, film killed vaudeville, and television killed bowling leagues, so did blogs allegedly kill journalism and mainstream media, replacing these with idiots and amateurs who failed to check their facts and ranted about their pet issues (as well as issues with their pets). There's a constant underlying all this killing – corporate power. Even as some media forms eclipse others, global conglomerates profit from the innovations while pernicious arrangements of state power benefit from a diverted populace. Television can't deliver the requisite eyeballs? No problem. Switch gears, locate other sites to capitalize. The dominance of capitalism as a system requires changes in industry; innovation drives capitalism. State forms adapt as well: disintegrated spectacles allow for ever more advanced forms of monitoring, tracking, and surveillance.[7] People plead for more cameras to keep them safe as they shop and happily relinquish personal data in exchange for saving a few cents here or there, for shaving seconds off this site or that.

The opposition of the death of the old and vitality of the new, as well as the concomitant cries to condemn the old ways and celebrate the new, is a recurrent theme in technology and media writing that tells us nothing about the technologies and media practices involved. Inserting new actors into old series, the opposition between old and new obscures the practices and settings of technologies, the ways technologies are used (ways that are often diverse, conflicting, and unexpected), and the ways these uses produce different sorts of subjects. For example, in the 1970s access to and knowledge of computing put one in an elite class of scientists and engineers. By the end of the 1980s, computer literacy was considered a core skill or competence. In the twenty-first century, spending time online is suspected to be as much of a time-waster as watching television.

Blogging's obituary, though, is not just premature. It's not just an error. Rather it alerts us to a change in a practice, a change that appears as an effect of our looking back. When bloggers are killers ushering in fundamental changes in media, politics, and journalism, they are understood within a logic of desire. That is, there is an underlying supposition that at some point in time some people wanted blogs, that blogs were objects of desire produced to fill a previous lack. For example, people didn't trust the mainstream media, so they starting blogging in order to produce a journalism they could trust. The shift to death rhetoric marks a move away from this economy of desire and toward one of drive. When blogs are situated in a logic of drive, they aren't something we want but lack, aren't something introduced into a lack that they can't fill. They are objects difficult to avoid, elements of an inescapable circuit in which we are caught, compelled, driven.[18]

In Lacanian psychoanalysis, desire and drive each designate a way that the subject relates to enjoyment. Desire is always a desire to desire, a desire that can never be filled, a desire for a *jouissance* that can never be attained. In contrast, drive attains *jouissance* in the repetitive process of not reaching it. Failure (or the thwarting of the aim) provides its own sort of success. If desire is like the path of an arrow, drive is like the course of the boomerang. What is fundamental at the level of the drive, Lacan teaches, is "the movement outwards and back in which it is structured."[19] Through this repetitive movement outward and back the subject can miss its object but still achieve its aim; the subject can "find satisfaction in the very circular movement of repeatedly missing its object."[20] Because failure produces enjoyment, because the subject enjoys via repetition, drive captures the subject. Slavoj Žižek writes,"drive is something in which the subject is caught, a kind of acephalous force which persists in its repetitive movement."[21] The subject gets stuck doing the same thing over and over again because this doing produces enjoyment. Post. Post. Post. Click. Click. Click.

Although Freud's thinking about drive changed over the course of his research, his view is typically rendered in terms of two drives, eros and thanatos, life and death, connection and separation. Lacan rejects this dichotomy, arguing that drive as such is death drive. Rather than involving some kind of primary homeostasis or equilibrium, drives are a destabilizing force, a force that persists, that exerts a pressure, without regard for the pleasure and well-being of the subject. As a persistence that is not for the sake of the subject, drive, then, has almost an undead quality. It is excessive, persisting beyond the ostensibly natural contours of life and death. In the Lacanian view, drive as death drive encompasses the way that even a drive for life results in paradoxes wherein saving life entails sacrificing it, pursuing life leads to risking it, and cherishing life looks like a bizarre fixation on morbidity. Turning back in on itself, turning into its opposite, the death drive is reflexive.

3

Blogs emerge out of the internet environment of the late 1990s, but not, as Geert Lovink points out, as the result of "a movement or event."[22] They are more like "a special effect of software." Blogs are retroactive effects of networked practices of storing and linking. In the words of the Digital Methods Initiative, they are "natively digital" and in this way kin to threads, tags, links, and search engines. They've also spawned their own natively digital offspring, most specifically the post as the primary unit designating a contribution (as opposed to the page, a key unit for print culture that makes little sense in a digital environment).[23]

Blogging's kinship with search engines is particularly close: the first blogs were responding to the same problems that led to the development of search engines – how can one find something in particular on the internet?[24] Already in the late nineties the internet was imbued with a fantasy of abundance.[25] Anything was possible. One could connect to anyone, say anything, find everything. The truth was out there. Locating something specific, though, was another question altogether. There seemed to be too much noise, too much chaos. Finding useful, not to mention reliable, information was a challenge.

The first blogs (twenty-three counted in 1999) were logs of websites, signposts left by a previous navigator to those who might want to follow his path, trace her links.[26] The compiler of the list, or blogger, presented links to sites or articles she found particularly noteworthy. What made the list most helpful was the blogger's commentary, the description of the site or explanation as to why a given link was included. Commentary was the valued-added, the new content that made the blog itself worth visiting. The commentary let blog readers – those looking for reliable guides as they made their way through the web – know whether they could trust the blogger. One shouldn't forget, though, that the first blogs were only first later, after bloggers were blogging.

Blogs and search engines emerged in the place of a missing "subject supposed to know" (a concept from Lacanian psycho-analysis).[27] Early searchers trying to make their way through the noise to find what they were looking for had to presuppose not only that what they wanted was out there (a promise of abundance) but that they could find it (a promise of access). Given the way abundance – *everything was out there* – made searching infinitely time-consuming, one needed help – sign-posts, indexes, catalogues, portals, editors, search engines. Before Google there were multiple projects and paths attempting to provide this help. Blogs and search engines are two such projects, two fillings-in of the place that emerged for a subject supposed to know.

What was the subject supposed to know supposed to know? Not just how to find information, but the truth of the searcher's desire. That is to say, those searching on the internet might not know what they actually want. They might call it one thing, but mean another. They might not know what they mean, not be able to put their desire into words. Search engines and blogs were established to occupy a place for the knower of our secrets, our desires, a place for one who would know what we wanted when we didn't really know ourselves.

This supposition of a subject supposed to know is manifest in several different ways. One is hysterical. Faced with poor returns from a search query, the searcher responds with frustration, *No! That's not it! There must be something else, something more, something better.* Another response is paranoid. There must be something or someone behind the scenes, collecting the data, distorting the results. *Someone is watching, collecting. Someone or something is looking for me.* The paranoid response, then, exposes a tension: one wants knowledge to be available, but one doesn't want to be known. One's expectations are structured through a fantasy of abundance – the truth is out there – while at the same time one wants to withhold an aspect of oneself; the whole truth is not out there; my truth, the truth of my desire, remains withheld. There is even a perverse response that, again, demonstrates the underlying supposition of a subject supposed to know. The pervert positions himself as the instrument or guarantor of knowledge, the one who can deal with contingency, who can build a better search engine, come up with a completely reliable algorithm, serve as the vehicle for realizing the fantasy of abundance.

Blogs and search engines are different approaches to the same problem, different occupations of the same place. They point, though, in different directions. Faced with the challenge of providing a trusted guide through a chaotic, indeterminable, changing field, search engines say "trust the algorithm." In contrast, blogs say, "trust doesn't scale." So while the former offers a reliability based in equations and crawl capacities, the latter says, know the knower. It focuses on the person providing the link, offering the searcher the opportunity to know this person and so determine whether she can be trusted. Social network sites refract the problem of trust yet again: if the issue with blogs is the credibility of the guide or writer, the issue for social network sites is trust in the audience, in the others who might be following me.

Of course, this description is too simple: like search engines, blogs are a technological application. For many commentators, the capabilities enabled by this application establish the definition of a blog: a collection of posts (each with its own permalink), appearing in reverse chronological order, time-stamped, and archived. Posts can be texts, images, audio, and video. They may feature links to other blogs and sites on the internet. They may offer visitors opportunities to comment.

In her brief 2002 introduction to blogs, Meg Hourihan observes how "newness" attaches readers to blogs. Because the newest posts appear first, readers can easily keep up-to-the-minute track of what's blogged. They don't have to search through a site looking for the most current information. It's right in front them, likely provided by an RSS feed or newsreader. This immediacy helps tie readers to a site as they follow developments in real time. Even more significant than immediacy for attaching readers to blogs are those features of the blog format that contribute to cross-blog connections and conversations. Thus Hourihan emphasizes the time stamp and the permalink as aspects of the blog format conducive to connectivity. "The linking that happens through blogging creates the connections that bind us," she writes. "Commentary alone is the province of journals, diaries, and editorial pieces."[28] Trust is more than code and reliability is more than expertise and credentialing. Blogging responds to the problem of finding what one wants by offering something like a relationship, a connection.

4

What is a blog, anyway? danah boyd criticizes the metaphors on which early answers to the question relied.[29] Not only does she point out the interests technology companies had in defining blogging, interests linked to efforts to build and market their product as well as set standards and expectations for what blogs would be and how they would function, but she also rightly attends to the role of early researchers who treated blogging in terms of genre. The most prominent metaphors in these early attempts to define blogging were journals and journalism.[30]

Some researchers followed the lead of hosting services such as LiveJournal in viewing blogs as personal diaries or easily updatable journals. This diary metaphor creates a problem, though. What's appealing about networked personal diaries electronically available for anyone to read? Why would any person whatsoever want to read anyone else's boring journal?

And if the journal isn't boring, what sort of exhibitionistic narcissist would inflict it on the entire world? Understood in terms of personal diaries, blogs seem but another aspect of the reality television craze, part of entertainment culture's preoccupation with celebrity.

Other researchers agreed with the mainstream media and depicted blogs as new forms of citizen journalism.[31] Whether they treat blogs as vehicles for local and on-the-ground reporting or as sites for the expression of individual opinions, these attempts to define blogs in terms of journalism open up a host of difficulties. The most apparent has been the failure of the vast majority of blogs to live up to the journalistic standards established for them. Bloggers generally lack the ethics and skills associated with professional journalism. Few do new and original reporting but instead remediate the findings of real journalists as they mix into them their own strident, often vicious, points of view. Approached as a genre, then, blogs turn out to be rather pathetic, at least from the perspective of the mainstream media.[32]

Together, the two metaphors of journal and journalism configure the practice of blogging in terms of a private and a public sphere, failing to analyze or even acknowledge the inaptness of a modern spatial division as a way of thinking about contemporary media and communicative practices. As of March 2010, Google's blogging service, Blogger (which it purchased from San Francisco-based Pyra labs in 2002), was still relying on the journals and journalism metaphors:

> Professional and amateur journalists use blogs to publish breaking news, while personal journalers reveal inner thoughts.
> Whatever you have to say, Blogger can help you say it.[33]

Given the problems that arise when blogs are viewed as a genre, boyd advocates viewing blogs as a medium, as more like radio or paper than a novel or opera. Blogs serve up content for an audience of anyone, perhaps a few of the blogger's friends, more likely for an uncertain number of strangers. As media, blogs change and evolve. They coexist and interlink with other media (print, video, telephony, etc.). To this extent, blogs are part of an open set of communicative practices and technologies. As the spamblogs enact, anything, any gibberish whatsoever, can be content. What is communicated, the content of blogs, is secondary or tertiary to the fact of communication.[34] In boyd's words, "Blogs emerge because bloggers are blogging."

Blogging is a medium for and practice of communication. Unlike mass media, it doesn't target an imaginary community of everyone (in the nation, state, or city). Unlike one-to-one technologies like the telephone or one-to-a-designated-list technologies like email, blogging doesn't presume to reach a designated recipient. Nor does it rely on real-time interactions, live feeds (although various forms of syndication can alert readers when a blog has been updated). Instead, the medium enables the production of content potentially accessible to anyone who happens to find it. Blogging opens possible encounters with the different and unexpected, whether in the form of the blogger's own reflection on what she posts or in the reactions of others.

Some of the officiants at blogging's premature funeral agree with boyd on the centrality of the form. Writing for an electronic magazine based in Australia, Guy Rundle compares blogs to the CB radio fad:

> As with CBs, what thrilled people with blogs was "the ecstasy of communication," the pure fact of being out there in the wide cyberworld – in other words, the form rather than the content. What stales the experience is what some have thought was its greatest attraction – its networked capacity, which makes everyone producer and consumer, and hence collapses the notion of an audience (since time does not expand, while blog numbers do).
>
> What most realize is that blogging is the illusion of connection, publishing into a void and thus doubly isolating.[35]

Rundle's claim for an "illusion of collection" relies on his elision of audience and communication. Yes, most of those who expected blogging to lead to fame and fortune, to make them respected pundits or highly paid authors, those who presumed that blogs were typed television, would likely have been disappointed. The evidence shows, however, that ever more people are driven to communicate with others, others who may even be themselves, through blogs.[36]

5

The essence of the blog is the post. The post gets the blog off the ground. And keeps it going. When posts stop, the blog dies. If the blog owner doesn't delete the entire blog, the posts may have an afterlife available to search engines as viable permalinks on persisting blogs or even archived somewhere along with the rest of the internet. Even if the entire blog is deleted, the fact that posts can be copied, pasted, and repeated, that they can drift and circulate throughout the information networks of communicative capitalism, gives them a kind of haunting permanence. Posts are blogs' immortal remainders, revenants that once released can never be fully contained. The capacity of posts to circulate endlessly means that even dead blogs persist as digital zombies.

What's in a post? Anything. Blogging subjectivity isn't narrativized.[37] It's posted. It's not told as a story but presented in moments as an image, reaction, feeling, or event. The post is a form that expresses mediality as such. Blogs, and even more so Twitter, catch oral communication in linear writing. Like a phone call or text message, a post attempts connection. Facebook friends similarly "poke" each other or leave short remarks on each other's walls. Unlike calls and text messages, though, blog posts are stored, archived, and accessible to virtually anyone. They are immediacy saved, conversations preserved. Posts persist as traces of their originators (whether the originators be individuals, groups, or machines), traces of the addition of something else.

The addition may be original – my voice, my image, my remix. I contribute to mark not simply the fact that I am here, that I have a view, but that I am engaging. I am participating in the construction and extension of a manner of being together. If my addition is a tag or link, it contributes to the force or impact of that which is tagged or linked, extending its viability. It's no wonder, then, that blogging services provide so many tools for counting: How many lifetime page views? How many last month? How many today? How many this hour? Which post generated the most hits? Which one accumulated the most links? These counts report what has been added. They count additions, the expansions and extensions that are blogging. The value added, then, stems purely from the being added.

Adding creates openings for new links or connections. Perhaps someone will respond. Perhaps the response will generate more posts, more responses, something like a relationship. This possibility infuses additions with feeling, makes them carriers and transmitters of affect. Of course, a response may not be a comment. It may be just a visit, registered as a page view and counted. Even when there is no discernible response, my addition, my post, remains, the opening it introduced ready and present, available as a trace of my past to those who may find it in the future.

Instead of judging blog posts as a literary form, it is more useful to consider them as a form of expression in between orality and literacy, or perhaps as a kind of "secondary orality," to use Walter Ong's term.[38] While the idea of secondary orality remained relatively unexplored at the time of Ong's death, his characterization of orally based thought includes attributes already key features of mobile, SMS, and online communication:

1   Thoughts are combined and points are made in ways that are additive rather than supportive; differently put, people string syntactic elements together with "and" rather than with subordinate clauses.
2   The elements of thoughts and ideas are aggregative rather than analytical (a contemporary example might be the slogans, clichés, and memes that catch on and stand-in for ideas and feelings that remain unexplored).
3   Ideas and points are frequently repeated.
4   Traditions are conserved (because little to nothing is written down, remembering is difficult; hence, not only do points need to be repeated but they need to be attributed to tradition).

5 Ideas are understood in terms of their connection with actual experience, with the lifeworld, rather than abstractly or within a more general analytic field (*if I don't know anyone who has been the victim of homophobic violence, then homophobic violence must not be a problem*).

6 Knowledge and ideas appear agonistically, polarized, as part of everyday struggle.

7 Ideas are treated in terms of empathy and its lack: that is to say, in an immediate and participatory rather than a distanced fashion.

6

While boyd is right to criticize reading blogs through the metaphors of journaling and journalism, understanding why these metaphors fail tells us something about blogging as a media practice. Yes, they fail because they focus on the content of blogs rather than the practice of blogging, an increasingly glaring and obvious mistake as ever more paid journalists blog, blogs are cited in mainstream journalism as evidence from ordinary people, bloggers appear in print and on television and radio, and internet content is delivered to mobile phones. The content focus can't keep multiply intersecting modes of communication in view. Additionally, rather than following the conventions of either journaling or journalism, blogging occurs in a space that opens up between them, when the news that matters is news of me and my opinion. More important, though, the metaphors of journaling and journalism fail because their focus on the content misses the changes in subjectivity and setting of which blogging is a part.

The journaling metaphor takes for granted the personal identity of the subject as diarist, an odd move given the likelihood that the blog is written pseudonymously.[39] As journaling, blogging appears as a technology of the self, a way of documenting, reflecting on, and hence managing oneself. Although this idea has some intuitive appeal, it is belied by the long history of self-writing. The reduction of blogging to journaling overlooks the immense historical variety in practices of writing and their relations to different kinds of selves. Presuming a kind of singularity of the practice of self-writing, moreover, this reduction takes as given the continuity of the self, as if the technologies of the self were somehow not productive, as if a self stood behind the technologies of its own writing.[40]

Michel Foucault describes some of the early practices of writing the self.[41] In first- and second-century Rome, writing contributed to an ascetic practice of training the self, of changing the character by positing another before whom one would feel a sense of shame. Here writing is not simply a method for recording one's thoughts or reflecting on one's actions. It is a way of making present one who is not there, of summoning a companion in the imagination in order to feel the pressure of the other's gaze. With the suppositions of an other and of shame before this other, first- and second-century Romans, Foucault argues, construe writing as a technique for changing the self, not simply for recording its thoughts or for reflecting on these thoughts. Writing is a training with effects on an individual's character and practice.

Foucault mentions the *hupomnemata*, individual notebooks that aided memory. These were records of readings, sayings, and thoughts, collections to be used for strength or sustenance when needed. Foucault explains that the *hupomnemata* contributed to the formation of the self for three main reasons: "the limiting effects of the coupling of reading with writing; the regular practice of the disparate that determines choices, and the appropriation which that practice brings about."[42] Reading was thought to orient the mind toward novelty, to lead one to forget oneself and become scattered and distracted. By writing, one could affirm a set of truths which would constitute not only an object upon which to reflect but a basis for action. Writing the fragments, in other words, enables the writer to subjectivize them, to make them his own, aspects of his specific identity.

Another kind of self-writing was correspondence, letter writing. The written letter enabled the author to make himself present to others when he was apart, at a distance. Focusing on Stoic and Epicurean practices, Foucault observes:

To write is thus to "show oneself," to project oneself into view, to make one's own face appear in the other's presence. And by this should be understood that the letter is both a gaze that one focuses on the addressee (through the missive he received, he feels looked at) and a way of offering oneself to his gaze by what one tells him about oneself. . . . The reciprocity that correspondence establishes is not simply that of counsel and aid; it is the reciprocity of the gaze and the examination.[43]

Letters did not need to be about anything in particular. As a technique of the self, they weren't highlighting major events but rather testifying to "the quality of a mode of being." Cicero, for example, was quite explicit about his affection for correspondence for its own sake, regardless of whether he had anything to say:

I prefer to write an empty letter than not to write at all.
This then is all I have for you, nothing new. "Why bother then to write?" And when we are together, and chatter away with whatever comes into our heads? Surely there is *some* value in *causerie*, in which the mere interchange of talk is agreeable, even if there nothing behind it.[44]

For Foucault, the ordinariness, the fact that nothing much has happened, is what is noteworthy. Review of the ordinary gave one insight into the kind of life one leads and thus was ideal to a practice of self-examination. We might also emphasize the way that expressing "whatever comes into our heads" creates an opening to another, an opportunity for connection. What matters, Cicero tells us, is less the content that enables connection than the connection itself. There is some value in *causerie*, or chat, a value attached to interchange.

While attentive to technologies of the self, Foucault is less concerned with technologies of writing.[45] Early written Latin used interpuncts to designate separations between words. As the Romans borrowed more letter forms and vowels from the Greeks, however, they adopted the Greek practice of *scriptura continua* or uninterrupted writing.[46] That is, their letters were spaced equally apart, regardless of the beginning and ending of words. *Scriptura continua* made retrieving information after it had been read difficult, to say the least.[47] Unlike the Greeks, moreover, the Romans did not use page numbers, foliation, or catchwords, and only rarely paragraphs, to ease the presentation of textual material. Perhaps because of the suspicion of reading that Foucault notes, Romans did not want to make reading any easier. Thomas N. Habinek makes the point more directly, arguing that the material difficulties associated with reading and writing "were convenient means of keeping literature in the hands of the well-to-do elite."[48]

For wealthy Romans, writing was generally dictation and reading was generally being read to.[49] The aristocratic writer relied on the hands and skills of another who was actually reading or writing. Well-educated scribes had the difficult task of making sense of written Latin. Reading was slow, painstaking, and likely often done aloud or in a low mumble. Vocalization made it easier to turn letters into language sounds and language sounds into meanings. To be sure, the use of scribes contributed to problems in authentication, problems addressed through the development of distinct personal styles in expression as well as the use of seals.[50]

Elite households often employed trained lectors who performed texts for assembled groups. Texts, then, provided opportunities for conversation and discussion; they were more than just the expression of an author. William A. Johnson writes:

> The odd format of the bookroll itself intersects with the fact that literary texts were commonly "read" in the sense of a small group listening to a "performance" by a reader. The strict – one wants to say obsessive – attention to continuous flow in the design of the ancient book interlocks with the idea that it was the *reader's* job to bring the text alive, to insert the prosodic features and illocutionary force lacking in the writing system. The continuous roll was "played" by the reader much in the way that we play a videotape or witness a stage performance. . . .[51]

Even personal letters were often copied, circulated, and read in groups, much like pamphlets or newspapers in later times. Reading in groups was a common practice, a social activity and type of entertainment. If self-writing was a technology of the self, it was a technology deeply interlinked with connection to an audience and community. Reading and writing, for the ancient Romans, had aesthetic elements tied to the pleasures of engagement with others.

7

Paul Saenger writes:

> Word separation can be regarded as a product of the frontier civilizations that had developed at the periphery of what had been the Roman Empire. Throughout history, intellectual, technical, and social innovations have often first appeared on the margins of well-established cultures. America and Japan can properly be regarded as frontier civilizations, the former of Europe, the latter of China. Although in the early Middle Ages the impetus for the restructuring of the page had come from the literary achievements of the empire's northern frontier, by the early tenth century the prominence of the Insular authors identified with word separation such as Bede, Alcuin, Sedulius Scottus, Johannes Scottus, and the anonymous compilers of glossaries had waned. A new corpus of scientific knowledge, and with it a new impetus for the adoption of word separation, sprang forth in another linguistic frontier zone, that of Mozarabic Spain.[52]

A product of globalization, blogging similarly emerges at the intersections of differing languages, cultures, and discourses, as the subsumption or folding into one another of their edges and frontiers.[53] The imagistic properties of texts that enable words to be seen as distinct units of meaning, as direct correspondents to objects and acts in the world, continue to intensify in this millennium as they did in the previous two. Can one easily glean or absorb or be impressed by a written word, be impressed so quickly that one hasn't quite read it? Can one quickly identify a link? Quickly ascertain the presence or absence of something new? Can one immediately discern the structure of the visual field so that one knows what not to read, where to put one's time or effort? Color, space, images – all these establish the visual fields of blogs.

8

Foucault's technologies of the self rely on the installation of a gaze, of the perspective of another before whom the subject imagines itself. In a first instance, the installation of this gaze can be thought of as the substitution of a symbolic position in the place of the audience of others customary in classical textual performances. For the subject this gaze constitutes an Other "who registers my acts in the symbolic network."[54] It provides the subject with an ego ideal, a point of symbolic identification. Žižek argues that this gaze is a crucial supposition for the subject's capacity to act. The gaze *qua* ego ideal is the point from which one sees one's actions as valuable and worthwhile, as making sense. Absent that gaze, one may feel trapped, passive, or unsure as to the point of doing anything at all. To this extent, identifying with the gaze enables the subject's activity.

The gaze structures our relation to our practices. For example, instead of experiencing the state as myriad forms and organizations, branches and edicts, presences and regulations, in our daily activities we tend to posit the state as a kind of entity, an Other aware of what we are doing. Similarly, we may posit an enemy assessing our every action. The point is that through symbolic identification the subject posits the very entity it understands itself as responding to. How it imagines this Other will be crucial to the kinds of activities the subject can undertake.

Weirdly, then, the active subject has to posit a kind of passivity: that is, a passive Other before whom the subject appears. The subject has to imagine himself, in other words, as fascinating the Other, as doing something or saying something or even watching something that captivates the Other. As Žižek emphasizes, the gaze is thus reflexive, doubled insofar as the subject sees itself being seen.[55] The one who is captivated, in other words, is the subject.

Although the subject needs to posit a gaze in order to understand its acts as mattering, registering, there is something disturbing about the gaze, something foreign and excessive, unchosen and unwanted. Žižek writes that "in the case of the gaze, the point to which the subject makes himself seen retains its traumatic heterogeneity and nontransparency, it remains an object in a strict Lacanian sense, not a symbolic feature."[56] In a setting of multiply interlinked media, we are never quite certain to what we have made ourselves visible. We don't know who is looking at us or how they are looking. We can't even be sure whether there is a single or multiple perspectives. What databases are we in? Who has googled us and why?

This disturbing uncertainty points to a second, more traumatic, version of the gaze, the gaze not as the big Other of the ego ideal but as what Lacan refers to as the small other, *objet petit a*. In this version, the gaze refers to our own entrapment in the field of the visible: "I see only from one point, but in my existence I am looked at from all sides."[57] What one sees is always incomplete, in need of being filled in. Yet this filling-in necessarily brings with it inadequacies and distortions. The subject might fill in what he wants to see; his desire may fill in the gaps he encounters. He may then become aware of such a gap and his involvement in it, feeling himself somehow seen, even vulnerable. Each side of this relation to the gap (to a lure or stain in the visible field) – the side of seeing it and of being seen seeing it – is an aspect of the gaze.

Joan Copjec's reading of Freud is one of the best accounts of the gaze. Freud's argument, she explains,

> distinguishes the act of looking at oneself through the intermediary of an *alien object* from the act of looking at oneself through an *alien person*. The first concerns that reflexive circuit by which one apprehends oneself in the categories of the culture to which one belongs or of someone one wishes to please, with the result that one thereby regards oneself as a known or knowable object. The second concerns a completely different kind of circuit, that of the active-passive drive, which turns around on itself. In this case, because I do not expose myself to the look of a determinate other, I do not receive a message back regarding my determinate identity. The reflexive circuit of scopic drive does not produce a *knowable object*; it produces a *transgression of the pleasure principle*, by forcing a hole in it. The scopic drive produces an exorbitant pleasure that disrupts the ego identity formed by the first circuit.[58]

I once thought I saw the postman sitting in his delivery truck cuddling a puppy. This seemed odd. A second glance revealed that he was sorting letters and that there was no puppy. I immediately felt embarrassed, even rather ashamed. It was almost as if there were a gaze in the postman–(missing) puppy complex that saw me see myself making this bizarre mistake. It felt like I was caught not just making the mistake but realizing the mistake. In Lacan's words, "Generally speaking, the relation between the gaze and what one wishes to see involves a lure. The subject is not presented as other than he is, and what one shows him is not what he wishes to see."[59] Gaze, then, refers not to a specific person whom one imagines being seen by but rather to a more unsettling feeling of an excess disturbing one's seeing, both in terms of what one sees and in one's being seen.

Some bloggers find themselves disoriented by the experience that people they know read their blogs. We presumed we were posting for strangers and ended up more exposed than we expected. Our families, friends, colleagues, or employers were lurking on our blogs, learning about our passions and idiosyncrasies. The audiences before whom we perform our identities – child, expert, collector, lover – converged, undermining the separations and distinctions that told us who we were, rendering us nothing in particular, but still something. Blogging is a technology uncoupled from the illusion of a core, true, essential, and singular self. The subjects of blogs are fragmented, appearing as neither true nor false, just appearing as whatever they happen to post.

More formally put, in communicative capitalism, the gaze to which one makes oneself visible is a point hidden in an opaque and heterogeneous network. It is not the gaze of the symbolic Other of our ego ideal but the more disturbing, traumatic gaze of a gap or excess, *objet petit a*. Our disclosures are surveilled, archived, remembered, in ways that exceed our ability to manage or control. On the one hand, this is the source of their immense attraction, what lures us in, what incites us to practices of revelation and display. On the other, the media that incite us to create and express, to offer our thoughts, feelings, and opinions *freely*, to participate (but in what?), deliver us up to others to use for purposes of their own.

Because one is never sure how one is seen, one is never certain of one's place in the symbolic order. How, exactly, are we being looked at? One never really knows who one is – despite all the cameras, files, media, and databases. A celebrity gamer in one place is elsewhere just another kid. A famous jazz musician may have zero name recognition among economists. Someone with a million friends on MySpace may be no one at all to the rest of us. Facebook tries to help us out with this by supplying endless quizzes that promise to tell us who we really are – which *Lord of the Rings* character, which famous philosopher, which ferocious animal. Who one is in the sociosymbolic order is uncertain – and ever-changing. The order is never fixed; it is in constant flux. Žižek tags this flux and uncertainty as a decline in symbolic efficiency.

In the terms of Lacanian theory, the decline of symbolic efficiency is accompanied by a convergence between the imaginary and the Real. Imaginary identities sustained by the promise and provision of enjoyment replace symbolic identities. The global information and financial networks of communicative capitalism offer new ways for us to imagine ourselves, immense varieties of lifestyles with which we can experiment. Each can and must be creative, different, unique. Each must develop a distinctive personal style. These unique identities, though, are extremely vulnerable. The frames of reference that give them meaning and value are constantly shifting. Challenges to these identities can appear at any moment. Others' successes, achievements, and capacities to enjoy too easily call our own into question. So while it may seem that the decline of symbolic efficiency ushers in a new era of freedom from rigid norms and expectations, the fluidity and adaptability of imaginary identities are accompanied by fragility and insecurity. Imaginary identities are incapable of establishing a firm place to stand, a position from which one can make sense of one's experiences, one's worlds. Blogs mark and mediate these identities, whatever they might be.

Social network sites respond to the decline of symbolic efficiency. Anxious before the gaze, before the disturbing inquiries and intrusions of unknown others, unsure about what to expect, about whether one is succeeding or failing, whether others are friends or foes, we build more reliable, apparently intimate networks. We may not know everyone in our intimate network, but we know they are friends – we had to friend them. Someone has vouched for them. We share a connection or have a connection produced for us by virtue of the games and gifts available on the site. With fewer strangers, these networks are less stressful that the open uncertainties disrupting our attempts to sense who we are or might be. There are people we can trust, people who share with us little moments of their day, assuring us that there might still be some reality that we have in common. Presenting our lives and activities to our network, we attempt to install in ourselves a capacity for action. Maybe that's why cyber-bullying emerged with such force in 2007: it's not that there weren't bullies before MySpace and Facebook (bloggers have always complained about trolls); it's that people continued to believe in and search for connection.

9

To emphasize the decline of symbolic efficiency is to emphasize a retreat from or effacement of the law of desire and an amplification of the logic of drive. The primary setting for our activity as communicating subjects is not law and its transgression but drive's repetitive circuit.

Žižek explains the difference between desire and drive via a change in the position and function of *objet petit a*. He writes:

> Although, in both cases, the link between object and loss is crucial, in the case of the *objet a* as the object of *desire*, we have an object which was originally lost, which coincides with its own loss, which emerges as lost, while, in the case of the *objet a* as the object of drive, the "object" *is directly the loss itself* – in the shift from desire to drive, we pass from the *lost object* to *loss itself as an object*. That is to say, the weird movement called "drive" is not driven by the "impossible" quest for the lost object; it is *a push to directly enact the "loss" – the gap, cut, distance – itself.*[60]

Drive is a kind of compulsion or force. It's a force that is shaped, that takes its form and pulsion, from loss. Drive is loss as a force or the force loss exerts on the field of desire.

The compulsive movement of drive shapes networked media as they enact the loss of symbolic efficiency. This enactment is not an effort to restore the symbolic. Rather, it's the "extraordinarily plastic" movement of the drives, to borrow Freud's expression. Freud continues, "They may appear in each others' places. One of them may accumulate the intensity of the other."[61]

That the drive is thwarted or sublimated means that it reaches it goal by other means, through other objects. Blocked in one direction, it splits into multiple vectors, into a network. If Freud views the process as akin to the flow of water into multiple tributaries and canals, we might also think of it as an acephalic power's attempt to constitute and reach its objects by any means necessary – and then to do it again and again and again and again, getting a little enjoyment in each repetition.

Lacan emphasizes that the drives are partial drives. He specifies this idea as "partial with regard to the biological finality of sexuality."[62] I understand the point to refer to the variety of changing, incomplete, and dispersed ways subjects enjoy. Drives do not develop in a linear fashion from infant to adult. They fragment and disperse as they satisfy themselves via a variety of objects. As Copjec writes, "It is as if the very function of the drive were this continuous opening up of small fractures between things."[63] Her language here is precise: the fractures are not of things but between them; the parts that are objects of the drives are not parts of wholes but parts that appear in the force of loss as new expressions of a whole. She uses Gilles Deleuze's example of the role of the close-up as a cinematic device: it's not part of a scene enlarged; rather, it's an expression of the whole of the scene.[64] Lacan refers to the partial object as an object of lack, an object that emerges in the void of the drive to provide the subject with satisfaction.

Correlative to the part is a further aspect of drive that Lacan renders as montage, a constant jumping without transition between heterogeneous elements. Montage suggests

movement without message, movement with intensity, movement outward and back. Disparate images and sounds shift
and mutate without beginning or end, head or tail. Lacan: "I
think the resulting image would show the working of a dynamo
connected up to a gas-tap, a peacock's feather emerges, and
tickles the belly of a pretty woman, who is just lying there
looking beautiful."[65] More contemporary ways to understand
montage are mash-ups, samples, and remixes – or, better, our
very movement through contemporary communication and
entertainment networks. I enter. I click. I like. I poke. Drive
circulates, round and round, producing satisfaction even as it
misses its aim, even as it emerges in the plastic network of
the decline of symbolic efficiency.

10

In the *Ethics of Psychoanalysis* Lacan positions drive between
the two deaths, symbolic death and the death of the organism.
Blogging after the death of the blogs persists in an analogous
domain of the drive. Caught in the circuits of communicative
capitalism out of which it emerged, it persists, whether in the
form of fully automated splogs, the remnants of past posts
excavated and ranked by Google, or our compulsions to make
ourselves seen.

3 Whatever Blogging

1

In 2007, e-commerce types were agog at the success of American teenager Ashley Qualls. By the time she was seventeen, she was making over a million dollars a year from Whateverlife.com, the busy pink website she designed to market MySpace page layouts. Market is not quite the right word, though. Her layouts and ad-ons weren't for sale. They were free. Her income came from advertising. Because Whateverlife.com gets more than sixty million hits a month, exceeding the circulation of several of the most popular English-language teen magazines combined, it supplies advertisers with a valuable commodity, the eyeballs of teenage girls. Qualls, or "AshBo" as she calls herself, started Whateverlife. corn in 2004. By 2007, she had expanded her site into something close to a community for girls, a go-to site where girls could find tutorials for making their own layouts as well as a variety of images, banners, captions, buttons, and boxes for decorating their MySpace pages. In addition to the revenue-generating ads, Whateverlife.com (with its growing staff of writers and designers) features a magazine and a link to AshBo's blog on her MySpace page.

Although Qualls' popularity is exceptional, her profile fits the dominant one for US bloggers: she is under thirty and female.[1] The Pew Internet and American Life Project report on Teens and Social Media provides some context: only 8 percent of adult internet users in the US have created a blog, but 28 percent of online teens blog, and these are most likely to be girls. Describing her site as "a place to express yourself,"

Qualls repeats the reason most US bloggers give for blogging, a wish to express herself creatively.[2] There were other rewards too, however. By 2007 she was earning enough from Whateverlife.com to drop out of high school and purchase a house.[3]

AshBo explains how she came up with the name for her site:

> WhateverLife.com is simply put as an "inside joke". It then developed into something else – as "For whatever life you lead" – meaning there would be information and fun things for anyone and everyone! (Which is why I'm always expanding in content . . . er, as much as I can!) [[[Or, for the long story . . . a night at Bre's back in 2004 (playing Mario Party 2 or 3 . . .) – we both lost to computer characters (I think DK was on EASY) – So I throw the controller down and walk off. On my way, I say "Whatever, Life" – as sarcastically as possible. Then I started thinking about how neat of a website name it would be. Here it is. :) ♥]]]

"Whatever" sprouts up all over the new media environment. Sightings include a blog by writer John Scalzi, a music video called "United States of Whatever," by Liam Lynch (as well as its remixes into cartoons of George W. Bush responding to comments that could suggest disagreement with his policies with the phrase "Whatever. This is my United States of whatever"), multiple home video clips of babies saying "whatever" on YouTube, and a show called *whatever with Alexis and Jennifer* on the Martha Stewart channel on Sirius satellite radio. The show features the "whatever girls," Stewart's daughter, Alexis, and her friend, Jennifer Koppelmann Hutt (the daughter of Stewart's producer). In addition to their radio show, the whatever girls have blogs, bulletin boards, and an online shop for buying "whatever" merchandise.[4] *Whatever* is also the title of a 1998 movie about teens in the pre-AIDS eighties (directed by Susan Skool) and an internationally acclaimed novel by Michel Houellebecq, published in French in 1988.

Ashley Qualls provides an image of blogging as a popular technological practice of content production, media use, and multiple platform integration inscribed into everyday life such that there is little difference between being on- or offline. Together with the statistical snapshots provided by the Pew

Internet and American Life Project, this image might let us feel like we are accessing a truth about blogs and social networks: they are by and for teenage girls. Both produce affective spaces where they express themselves, share their feelings, and reach out with a little hope that someone will be touched and reach back. Accessed through the intense emotional world of networked adolescence, blogs aren't confined to a sphere separate from other media. They are situated in a rich communicative habitat consisting of multiple platforms and applications (mobile phones, social network sites, video, music, and photo sharing sites). Blogs seem, then, to be ways that anyone of us could report on, share, experience, and even market our social lives. With a little luck, we could even earn revenue on ads accompanying each and every heartfelt expression. Feelings can be profitable.

2

The image constituted through the combination of statistics and the experience of a single blogger is too easy, even as it highlights the juxtaposition between the singular and the many characteristic of contemporary networked media. Rather than relying on one to stand in for an impossible whole, we do better to consider the rise of personalized media as a mass phenomenon and practice. By 2008, there were from eighty to a hundred and twenty million blogs.[5] The overwhelming majority of these blogs appear and die in a matter of months, having been seen by few if any readers. Blogs are many and innumerable, an open, changing, set of unique expressions. At the same time, the standardization supplied by blog services – the basic page layouts, archival features, titles, banners, ads, and widgets – formats blogs as ultimately interchangeable, the same, one virtually indistinguishable from another.

An easy test: from the Blogger dashboard (www.blogger.com), click on the "next blog" link; repeat again and again. You'll move through various blogs in various languages, seemingly at random. I've encountered blogs featuring photos of horse hoofs and how to care for them, travel photos, old watches, pie recipes, wedding preparations. On my screen, configured within Blogger's range of possible layouts, the blogs blend into and substitute one for another.

The common format that makes blogs blogs is a condition for the unique productions of singular bloggers. And vice versa: without the unique offerings, indeed, the promise that each voice can be heard, each experience documented, each opinion expressed, blogging has no point.

We can approach this same entanglement from a different direction: blogs offer exposure and anonymity at the same time. As bloggers we expose ourselves, our feelings and experiences, loves and hates, desires and aversions. Yet we often write as if we've opened ourselves to nearly no one, to just a select few, to a small community of those we trust, perhaps because we cannot see them. Knowing full well that we are one among millions, we may find ourselves relieved not to have so many hits, so many comments. Strangers and opponents remind us of our exposure, our visibility, vulnerability, and ultimate lack of control.

After I gave a talk as part of a symposium on evil at MIT, a neo-Nazi found my blog, *I Cite*. He wrote:

> You live in an environment where debate is not free, and your half-witted ideas are protected and allowed an existence that exposure to reason would not accord them. . . . You imply here that you are being criticized because you criticized Bush. No. You are being criticized because you sounded stupid while criticizing Bush. . . . God, what do you think of the world? Do you think there are some politically-correct blog police that are going to stop people from criticizing you, like they do at your university? In the United States there is a First Amendment, and just like the First Amendment allows you to prattle on like a moron with vapid ideas that no real person takes seriously, it allows people to point out that your ideas are vapid and you're prattling on like a moron. Not everyone has to be nice to you; not everyone has to agree with you; and your extreme pathological reaction to criticism is disturbing. You are not fully developed psychologically, and I strongly recommend you quit your job and go out into the real world to toughen up a bit, because if you can't debate a few easy criticisms, at some point, the real world will eat you. Even the moron claiming I'm a racist slumlord is doing better than you.

I didn't respond. I didn't know how to. It's as if his remarks momentarily shattered the presumptions and expectations that enabled me to write so openly, exposing their specificity, their fragility, their context dependency, confronting me with the fact that my fantasized audience was not my real one.

Blogs can be useful political tools: they let activists report on their activities, plans, and aspirations. They help them meet up and coordinate. At the same time, they deliver a lot of knowledge to activists' opponents, the university officials wanting to know which students are responsible for the sit-in, the law enforcement officials trying to diminish the impact of planned demonstrations, to discourage activists from *going too far*. Privacy and consumer protection advocates remind us of the accumulation of data on consumers, data easily mined for the sake of the increasingly specific and personalized targeting of ads. Yet this information in need of protection is the open content of millions of blogs and social network profiles. Blogs make monitoring easy. *There's no need to spy! I'll tell you everything . . . and more!* In short, blogging relies on a fantasy of exposure without exposure correlative to the indistinguishable mass of the singularly unique. It's like the thrill of telling a secret without being burdened by anxiety over its being told – exposure without exposure.

Social networks like MySpace and Facebook deploy a similar fantasy – one can share one's life with one's friends without repercussion. On the one hand, because one has specifically friended those in one's network, one can rest assured that one's secrets are safe. *If you can't trust your friends, who can you trust?* On the other, the drive to grow one's network (*Look! I'm somebody! I've got thousands of friends – they like me; they really like me!*), to friend people with whom one works, people from different parts of one's life, belies the illusion of control over one's personal information. Not only is one's data shared with third parties, but the surveys and games that flourish in social network environments expand third-party access: access to my friend is a way of getting access to me. A typical Facebook profile reveals a person's name, age, birthday, location, occupation, high school and/or university, relationship status, sexual orientation, political affiliation, religion, and personal appearance. Add to this the fact that most users mention events they attend, groups to which they belong, causes they support, and the result is a heavy degree of exposure.[6]

Typically, we respond to these seemingly paranoid lines of thought with deflection –it isn't *me* about whom data is collected; it's us – an aggregate. It's *our* patterns, not *mine*. It's how many of *us* refer to a new movie or click on an ad, not whether *I* do. As with blogging, our participation in social networks relies on the supposition that we expose but are not exposed, that we are unique but ultimately indistinguishable.

3

Developing a notion offered by Giorgio Agamben, Dominic Pettman considers the problem of the interchangeable yet irreplaceable in terms of "whatever being." For Pettman, as for Agamben, whatever being points to new modes of community and new forms of personality anticipated by the dissolution of inscriptions of identity through citizenship, ethnicity, and other modern markers of belonging. Describing the character actor as exemplary of whatever being, Pettman glosses the concept as "an enactment of existence without qualities, or at least qualities so interchangeable and obvious that they erase all identity." In positive terms, whatever being is a tag for the "sheer generic potentiality of being."[7]

Agamben emphasizes that the "whatever" in whatever being relates not to singularity as indifference to a common property "but only in its being *such that it is*." He writes:

> In this conception, such-and-such being is reclaimed from its having this or that property, which identifies it as belonging to this or that set, to this or that class (the reds, the French, the Muslims) – and it is reclaimed not for another class nor for the simple generic absence of any belonging, but for its being-*such*, for belonging itself. Thus being-*such*, which remains constantly hidden in the condition of belonging ("there is an *x* such *that* it belongs to *y*") and which is in no way a real predicate, comes to light itself: The singularity exposed as such is whatever you *want*, that is lovable.[8]

There is belonging, but not to anything in particular. Something in particular is insofar as it belongs. Asking "to what?," Pettman and Agamben suggest, mistakenly prioritizes the set over the very condition of belonging. What matters is belonging, not that to which one belongs.

At the same time, "mattering" triggers an intervention into what could seem little more than another way of designating indifference. Mattering matters. It's the interjection or scission of love and desire, of *wanting*. What matters stands out from the mass or multiple because it matters. As Pettman suggests, that I love it, desire it, separates it from the endless, open, uncountable set of indistinguishable members.

There are over a hundred million blogs. At least one of them is mine.

4

In US popular vernacular, "whatever" is an affective, verbal response that deflects another's comment. It is generally uttered in response not to a question, but to a statement or observation through which another might be attempting to harness the recipient or hearer.

"You haven't cleaned your room." "Whatever."

One of multiple video mash-ups of Liam Lynch's punk-pop "Whatever" combines images of George W. Bush and his vice president, Dick Cheney, Lynch's guitar tracks, and a Bush-impersonation voice-over. Bush yells:

> I'm George W. Bush, leader of the free world. I want to bomb Iraq. And when the world says, "no!" I say, "whatever!"
> Saddam has started to meet our demands. Yeah, whatever.

He sings the refrain, "'cause this is my United States of whatever."

The response "whatever" registers the fact of another utterance, of a communicative effort or engagement. It acknowledges communicativity through the deflection of the communicative effort. The sender's message (whether understood in terms of its content or its intent, whether conscious or unconscious) is neither accepted nor rejected. Rather, the "whatever" response distills the message into the simple fact of utterance.

"Whatever" resembles the response of Herman Melville's "Bartleby," the scrivener who replies "I would prefer not to" when given a task or instruction.[9] For some contemporary philosophers (for example, Michael Hardt and Antonio Negri), Bartleby provides a figure of refusal, opposition, or resistance, a model of escape or disentanglement from the relations of power constitutive of contemporary capitalist control societies. The argument is premised on power's dependence on resistance: the transgression of the law calls law into being. Or, protestors need police brutality in order demonstrate the validity of their protests. Bartleby, then, suggests a way out of the dialectic of law and its transgression. Side-stepping resistance, he deprives power of its hold.

Yet even as Bartleby evades the circuit of power and resistance by refusing to refuse, he continues to rely on his position as a singular subject: he says "I," referring to himself as a subject, and not just any subject, but a subject with a view, a preference. As such, he remains exposed to power. He still cares. In response to a request, Bartleby does more than acknowledge communication, the fact that a message has been delivered and received. His answer affirms the intelligibility of the request even as it challenges the normative expectations informing it. And rather than challenging the sender of the message's authority to make the request he makes, Bartleby asserts himself as what matters – *he* would prefer not to. He is a subject with preferences, and these preferences must be attended to.

In contrast, the only affirmation in "whatever" is of communication as such. Another has communicated. This communication in no way obligates me as the recipient of the message. By responding "whatever," I have signaled the minimum degree of awareness of communicative being: a message is sent in expectation of a response (after all, I didn't completely ignore you). "Whatever" asserts no preferences. It neither affirms nor rejects. And it doesn't expose the subject as a desiring subject to whom something matters.

There is also an affective dimension to "whatever," an insolence or attitude or provocation that arises out of its function as a non-responsive response. By acknowledging communication without attending to the content of the message, "whatever" denies the sender the sense that her message has been received because its content remains unaddressed. The sender is challenged, her position as sender undermined. "Whatever" forestalls a communicative exchange even as it adopts communicative form. It refrains from establishing the subject position of the one who responds with "whatever," and it unsettles the position of the one who initiates the exchange. It's a glitch in orality.

If communicativity such that it is, whatever communicativity, tags forms of subjectivity and belonging discernible in contemporary media practices, who and what is likely to benefit? What kinds of political and economic relations are likely to flourish in these new communicative habitats?

Whatever it takes.

5

By now an extensive literature exists documenting the production of national identities through media and communication technologies. Susan Buck-Morss's *Dreamworld and Catastrophe* is one of the best contributions to this research. Buck-Morss explores the mass identities of utopian and project-based states such as the United States and the Soviet Union during the twentieth century. She highlights the dreams and fantasies enabled by the movies, the imaginings of collectivity that film incited. For communists and capitalists alike, twentieth-century technological projects were also identity projects. Four components of Buck-Morss's account are particularly compelling: mass media's direct addressing of society; the way mass media change the nature of crowds; the spectacular function of mass media; and the compensatory logic of mass media's organization of space.

First, many have noted the ways mass media address, well, masses. Radio brought leaders' voices directly into people's homes, integrating leaders into their intimate spaces. Broadcast television likewise occupied a domestic space as it addressed its audience as personal members of a nation, perhaps imagined like a family (respected newscaster Walter Cronkite was affectionately referred to as "Uncle Walt"). But film in particular, with its large screen and grand scale, organized and spoke to the masses as a collective. The nation as national society is produced through the media address (whether newspaper, radio, television, or film), with no existence as such prior to this address.

Second, in a nuanced reading of the role of film production in the US and USSR during the 1930s, Buck-Morss observes,

> Whereas the radio voice allowed mass identification with political leaders, cinema, traveling to towns and villages to meet audiences halfway, represented a moving image of the masses that allowed audiences to recognize *themselves*. Such mirroring can be important in transforming the accidental crowd (mass-in-itself) into the self-conscious, purposeful crowd (the mass-for-itself), with at least the potential of acting out its own destiny.[10]

Unlike the moving carnival, whose spectators aggregate and disperse, cinema organizes, locates, and seats its spectators. Their attention is directed to a single place, to the screen. The unity of the screen produces out of the disunity of persons a singular audience that can see and recognize itself as a collective: "we" are watching this movie. For the Soviets, the films of Sergei Eisenstein played a particularly powerful role. Eisenstein captured and glorified intense scenes of revolutionary masses, images that became the memories of the October Revolution. Buck-Morss writes, "The particular characteristics of the screen as a cognitive organ enabled audiences to see the materiality not only of the new collective protagonist, but also of other ideal entities: the unity of the revolutionary people, the idea of international solidarity, the idea of the Soviet Union itself."[11] Similarly, in the United States, cinema changed the nature of the crowd by providing an imaginary mass body. In the early twentieth-century US, ethnic groups, religions, political organizations, and racist law worked against the image and goal of a unified political identity. Film countered these forces, offering massive cinematic bodies as points of singular identification. It was a crucial vehicle for mass assimilation via the production of a common culture and collective experience.[12] And as Buck-Morss emphasizes, the potential power of this new collectivity was enormous, whether as a force of production, consumption, or politics.

Third, Buck-Morss points out the potential for manipulation in cinema. In an argument reminiscent of Guy Debord's critique of the society of the spectacle, she notes how both Hollywood and Soviet cinema "affirmed official culture and denied certain bleak realities of social development."[13] The former presented dream versions of commodity consumption. Monumental stars, awesome production numbers (Busby Berkeley) and special effects (King Kong), and luxurious lifestyles captivated Depression-era audiences and attempted to channel their desire toward fantasies of consumption. The latter idealized production. Although Soviet film in the twenties continued the avant-garde experimentation of the revolutionary period (which was itself heavily influential in the US) even as it imported Hollywood movies, by the thirties socialist realism and the glorification of collective projects was culturally dominant. The chief of Soiuzkino (Soviet Cinema), Boris Shumiatskii, rejected Soviet art cinema as overvaluing formalism and aesthetics. A better model for socialist realism could be found in Hollywood, which employed a factory-like model of artistic production and a realistic style of "joyful spectacles" accessible to the masses.[14] One of the most successful Soviet films of this period was *Chapaev*, an action movie about the defeat of the White Russians in the Civil War that out-Western-ed the Hollywood movies it was modeled on.

Finally, the fourth aspect of Buck-Morss's discussion of the role of film in the production and imagining of mass national identities important for my argument is the division between public and private spheres. Here the Soviet and US cultural imaginaries are inversions of each other: the space that for one was a fantasized site of fulfillment was for the other a site of drudgery. "The forced intimacy of the communal apartment was a particular kind of terror affecting the most banal practices of every day," Buck-Morss explains. Insofar as public life under Stalinism was itself presented as the location of purpose and fulfillment, "there was no need for retreat into a private domain."[15] Conversely, in the US, factory work generally appeared as a particularly brutal, humiliating, kind of labor. Workers were subjected to control, subjection, the daily constraints and degradations of the assembly line. Rather than a source of fulfillment, industrial work was necessary drudgery. In return, workers received compensation in the form of consumption, enjoying consumer goods in the context of the love and warmth of the nuclear family. Buck-Morss writes, "the ideology of the private home came to bear a tremendous burden, that of legitimating the entire system of industrial capitalism, and nowhere more so than in the United States."[16]

6

What fantasies, what possibilities, what kinds of subjects, do multiply intersecting and increasingly personalized media and communication technologies stimulate? Differently put, how might changes from the media constitutive of projects of national utopian imagination lead in the direction of whatever beings? The pleasures of parallels with Buck-Morss's discussion of film and national mass identities suggest that answers might be found in at least four domains.

First, if mass media addressed society directly, organizing and speaking to masses as collectives, contemporary networked communications have multiple addressees, addressees known and unknown, friends and strangers. Bloggers may write for others whom they imagine share their interests, a group of the uninformed they might enlighten, or future versions of themselves. The set of friends who receive my updates on Facebook, my network, are uniquely mine. Each user's network is different, even as they overlap and intersect. Blogs and social networks do not provide broadly shared symbolic identities from which we see ourselves. Blogs don't address society writ large. They invite singular readers to consider what they have on offer. Or they just make themselves available to be found by search engines' crawlers. Unlike mass media's calling of collectives, publics, and nations into being, blogs don't unite bloggers and readers. To this extent, they are more like pencils than cinema. They remain specific in their multiplicity.

Second, whereas mass media made crowds visible to themselves as a unity, providing the crowd with an imaginary collective body, networked communication and entertainment makes particularities visible to themselves as particularities. I can tweet my current location, update my friends on my current mood, check what's trending. With multiply convergent and turbulent media, I don't have to settle on any one direction or theme. I can live in the momentary. Not only do these multiple, circulating impulses incite in me a kind of permanent indecision or postponement, a lack of commitment – *what else is out there?* – but the fragmenting, networking, thrust of drive turns my particular body, my very face, into a montage: a wrinkle here, a bump there, a nose too large, lips too small. Fortunately, I can update my photo at any time – and I can animate it, too! There is no us. There is no me (although I can google myself to see if I turn up). Buck-Morss argues that "Cinema creates an imagined space where a mass body exists that can exist nowhere else."[17] My point is that blogs – standing in for the networked information and entertainment media of communicative capitalism – not only do not create such a space for a mass body but dissolve any sense of it. They dis-place it, producing instead ever-accelerating circuits of images, impulses, fragments, and feelings. Blogs cannot be counted; they resist inclusion into sets or categories. Yes, cinema still exists and sometimes it lets us feel ourselves as something like an us . . . and then I can tweet about it. Blog mapping projects attempt to make multiple disparate blogs appear as a sphere, a collective, as points in a shared space. But the space they map is in the imaginary of the researcher, not in bloggers' presence to themselves as a collective.

Third, the cinematic spectacles produced by Hollywood and the Soviet Union in the 1930s generally sought to affirm official culture and deny the grimmer aspects of economic and social life. In contrast, blogs persist in a setting of total mediality: anything can be found, said, seen on the internet. With publicity as the ideology of communicative capitalism, everything can be said; nothing need be denied. Every aspect of contemporary life is reflected upon, criticized, mocked – and then the reflections, criticisms, and mockeries are themselves reflected upon, criticized, mocked . . . *did we go too far?* In this setting, nothing is unworthy of comment or commentary. Every aspect of the ordinary and everyday matters to someone – *for like a second.* Blogs say that whatever happens to me matters – in and of itself. And in this reflexive environment, even the fact that my posts are boring, that the arguments in my little segment of the blogipelago have an intensity far beyond merit, that the escapades of celebrities captured by TMZ are trivial, even all these facts are known and discussed. Most of the time, the repetitive intensities of blog drama are inversions of politics, rapidly circulating differences and modulations that ensure that nothing changes. Sometimes the intensities accumulate, "punctuated by catastrophic events, which are both creative and destructive."[18] Markets boom and bust; terrorists attack; a children's book becomes a global sensation. The circuits adjust and recalibrate, capturing the new again in the snares of communicative capitalism.

Fourth, just as the official myth of fulfillment through factory labor collapsed with the end of Stalinism (people didn't have to pretend anymore that it was true; they still had to go to work), the myth of idealized domesticity crumpled in the US, in part because of the achievements of feminism, in part because the realities of divorce, infidelity, addiction, and abuse made its fantasy impossible to sustain. Television and feminism both made the personal political, erasing the fragile and imaginary boundaries between public and private, a line that made little sense after the rise of the social. In the remnants of the myth of idealized domesticity, ideals of individual freedom and creativity are promoted. Personal satisfaction takes the place of familial duty. Differently put, family life is supposed to be *personally* rewarding (rather than a duty or expectation). When family life fails to satisfy, it is examined and diagnosed, offered remedies and supplements – the family *better* succeed because the brutal competition of neoliberalism offers neither shelter nor respite. Communicative capitalism provides the form and vehicle for the individualized consumption, participation, and creative needs expression of subjects compelled to be personally satisfied.

Correlative to the erasure of the always tenuous distinction between the public and private spheres is the dissolution of the boundary between work and play. From the initial electronics boom in the seventies through the larger shifts associated with personal computers and the internet, informatization has promised those who work with symbols and ideas increased ease and comfort. Early versions celebrated tele-commuting and the paperless office. Later versions preyed on fears of being left behind, out of the loop, not as quick as the competition. Consultants urged corporations to restructure work, to encourage creativity and team-building, to make work more like play. At the same time, with ever more games and interactions moving online, onto screens, play seemed a little more like work. In the circuits of communicative capitalism, the repetitions of drive suggest work without work (in the forms of work without pay or work that is fun) and play without play (in the forms of play for which one is paid and play for which one pays with enjoyment). This, then, is the setting wherein blogs are not escapes from the drudgery of part of one's life. They are not fantastic experiments in virtual reality. Rather, blogs instead extend out from, amplify, and reflect on whatever aspect of whatever life.

7

The change marked by the end of the Cold War has been tagged the end of ideology, the end of the Keynesian welfare state, the decline of the Fordist model of production, and the beginning of globalization, the information age, the network society, communicative capitalism. In their account of the new formation, Michael Hardt and Antonio Negri accentuate the passage from disciplinary society to the society of control.

Focusing on the capitalist societies of the US, UK, and Europe, they point out how disciplinary logics worked primarily within the institutions of civil society to produce subjects. By the end of the twentieth century, these mediating institutions – the nuclear family, the prison, the school, the union, and the local church – were in crisis. The spaces, logics, practices, and norms previously coalescing into social and economic institutions have broken down and apart. Their efficacy is now indeterminate. In other words, in some instances, the release of an institutional logic from its spatial constraints has given it all the more force; in other instances, the opposite has occurred.

Corresponding to this pervasive dissolution and indeterminacy (which itself necessarily correlates with the economic changes of informatization and the ubiquitous spread of networked communications) is an "indeterminacy of the *form* of the subjectivities produced."[19] Hardt and Negri argue that the old political subject – the citizen-subject of an autonomous political sphere, the disciplined subject of civil society, the liberal subject willing to vote in public and then return home to his private domesticity – can no longer serve as a presupposition of theory or action. Racial, ethnic, and sexual identifications are similarly less fixed, less stable, less available as determinate subject positions. In their place, we find fluid, hybrid, and mobile subjectivities who are undisciplined, who have not internalized specific norms and constraints, and who can now only be controlled.

Expressed in psychoanalytic terms, symbolic identity is increasingly meaningless in the society of control. What we have instead are imaginary identities sustained by excess *jouissance*, by an injunction to enjoy. More specifically, symbolic identity involves the subject's identification with an ego ideal, a perspective before whom the subject sees himself and his actions. Imaginary identification refers to the image that the subject adopts of himself. Symbolic identification, we might say, establishes the setting that determines which images appear and how it is that some are more compelling or attractive to us than others. Imaginary identification refers only to my self-image.

In disciplinary society, normative expectations coalesced around determinate social roles. Presuming the gaze of the school, church, family, or state, one could imagine oneself in different positions, positions that would either comply with or transgress institutional norms. I can be a conscientious student, faithful believer, dutiful daughter, good citizen. And, I can also be a delinquent, back-sliding, worthless, traitor. Even as the images differ, the symbolic identity of the gaze remains the same. In the wake of the decline of symbolic efficiency, the dissolution of disciplinary society, this gaze loses its prior force. We aren't sure if it's operative, if others believe it: is the good student a cog, uncreative, *thinking inside the box, a goody-two-shoes?* Does the Other actually admire and applaud transgression, and if so is it then more transgressive not to be transgressive since that's what the Other wants? Encountering the endless possibilities of contemporary reflex-ivity, post-disciplinary subjects are propelled to move through a variety of imaginary identities. We imagine ourselves one way, then another, never sure of how we appear because we don't know before whom we appear.

Lacking the ability to imagine how we appear to another, how another sees us, we lose the capacity to take the position of another, to see or think from another's perspective. We can choose any identity, but we lack the grounds for choosing or the sense that an identity, once chosen, entails bonds of obliga-tion.[20] Rather than following norms – Which ones? How do *they* know? Who made *them* the expert? – we cycle through trends, whether these come from fashion, diet advice, or the hope for an anchor in a particular subculture. A striking example of the dissolution of norms in the inability to take the perspective of another is regularly performed on amateur talent shows like *American Idol, Britain's Got Talent,* and *So You Think You Can Dance?* Upon hearing a judge's negative assessment of his or her performance, the contestant says something to the effect of "Well, that's just your opinion; I know I have talent." The oddness is that this response seems rooted in a failure to understand the very practice of judging and competition in talent shows. At any rate, the society of control places limits on the mobility and fluidity of contemporary hybrid identities, but these limits are not those installed by a Master signifier or symbolic law. To this extent, they are experienced by subjects as either groundless intrusions, irrational barriers to enjoyment (the *American Idol* version: Simon Cowell is simply cruel), or as hypothetical or instrumental injunctions, as means for achieving enjoyment later. Caught in reflexive networks – always another move, another level – we lose the capacity for reflection. Our networks are reflexive so that we don't have to be.

We are not bloggers. We are not Facebook. The networked interactions of communicative capitalism do not provide symbolic identities, sites from which we see ourselves as loci of collective action. Rather, they provide opportunities for new ways for me to imagine myself, a variety of lifestyles that I can try and try on. This variety and mutability makes my imaginary identity extremely vulnerable – the frames of reference that give it meaning and value are forever shifting; the others who can rupture it might appear at any moment and their successes, their achievements, their capacities to enjoy call mine into question: *I could have had more; I could have really enjoyed.* This insecurity is not only psychic; it's a reasonable response to struggles to persist in global, reflexive financial and information networks. Most of the economic benefits of neoliberal capitalism – of the new economy celebrated by digital media gurus – follow a power law distribution. A lucky few will get nearly everything. Most will get very little, almost nothing.

Hardt and Negri describe the ungovernable, mobile, and fluid singularities arising in the aftermath of disciplinary subjectivity in terms of an anthropological exodus. Hence, they emphasize that "those who are against" Empire's exploitation and domination "must also continually attempt to construct a new body and a new life."[21] Communicative capitalism facilitates and incites these attempts, employing ever innovative upgrades to ensure not just that the attempts continue but that they accelerate. Hardt and Negri acknowledge that the methods of anthropological exodus are the methods of Empire. But they don't accept that their response is also Empire's: do more, go further, radicalize, create something new, make tools into prostheses, migrate and mutate into information technologies. They write, "The will to be against really needs a body that is completely incapable of submitting to command."[22] An undisciplined body incapable of submission is a body of immediacy and enjoyment, driven to move from image to image, intensity to intensity. Lacking discipline, how can it resist, how can it form a will at all? Far from constructing something new, such a body forecloses the possibility and hope of self-governance.

Networked media in the society of control amplify the challenge postfordism poses to collective identity. Yes, they enable people to sign petitions. Yes, they enable people to give money. Yes, they enable people to express their opinions. Yes, *Obama had like a million Facebook friends.* But these particular motions of clicking and linking do not produce symbolic identities: they are ways that I express myself – just like shopping, checking my friends' updates, or following tabloid news at TMZ.com. I may imagine others like me, a virtual local, but this local remains one of those like me, my link list or followers, those who fit my demographic profile, my user habits. I don't have to posit a collective of others, others with whom I might need to cooperate or struggle, to whom I might be obliged, others who might place demands on me. The instant connection of networked association allows me to move on as soon as I am a little uncomfortable, a little put out. Petitions, social network groups (the one on Facebook that aims to get a million people to say they oppose capitalism has 24,672 members), blogs – they are the political equivalent of just in time production, quick responses circulating as contributions to the flows of communicative capitalism. In her compelling analysis of flash mobs, Cayley Sorochan takes the argument even further. Countering enthusiastic appropriations of flash mobs as new instances of democratic engagement, Sorochan presents them as instances of the "fetishizing of pure participation removed from any meaningful political project." She concludes, "Hopes that flash mobs might represent a future form of political organization reflect a desire for a politics of convenience where getting together with others is easy and does not involve conflict, commitment and struggle."[23]

In the circuits of communicative capitalism, convenience trumps commitment.

8

Agamben affiliates whatever being with the capitalist commodification of the human body and the technologization of its image in the spectacle.[24] The photographic images proliferating out of advertising and pornography are "neither generic nor individual, neither an image of the divinity nor an animal form." In them, the body "now became something truly *whatever*." The "whatever" Agamben invokes here suggests a new approach to Guy Debord's society of the spectacle, one that takes back from the spectacle the positive properties of being in language and being in common that it expropriates. For Agamben, whatever being is the mode of being in the coming community. Produced in capitalist spectacle, whatever being is a harbinger of a better future, one wherein the division held together in the unity of the spectacle is ultimately overcome. Because he wants to wrest transformations of human nature from their entrapment in the spectacle, Agamben suggests as an apposite image the "geometrical splendor" of the legs of a long line of dancing girls.

Another way to think about the idea of "neither generic nor individual" is to link it to the normalizing, aggregating aspect of disciplinary power. Modern disciplinary institutions, be they home, school, factory, or state, produced individuals as types, as occupants of social roles or positions. Recall photographs of Levittown, of soldiers in training, of graduates in their caps and gowns. The self-governing, reflective subject idealized as the outcome of the disciplines may have understood himself to be an individual, but more than that, he was an instance of a form. Autonomy appeared through individuality.

Agamben associates the planetary petty bourgeoisie with a frustration with and impropriety toward identities rooted in physical particularities or differences in language, tradition, or culture. He concedes that fascism and Nazism had already recognized in the petty bourgeoisie the "decline of the old social subject."[25] He jumps quickly over their nationalism as a false popular identity, though, as he asserts a new planetary refusal of identity.

With this jump, Agamben omits the mass as a modern collective force that is also neither generic nor individual. The mass is a displaced mediator between the planetary bourgeoisie and whatever being. In Jean Baudrillard's formulation, "The mass is without attribute, predicate, quality, or reference."[26] Agamben's whatever beings appear as singularizations of the mass. Bereft of qualities of their own, they are not the same as the mass resolved into its components: masses were masses of subjects, combinations and aggregations and accumulations of people across and against modernity's attempts to separate and order them. If the mass results from a combination of bodies that omits their specificities, whatever being skips the step of amassing to treat the indistinction, the without-qualities, not as a result of belonging to the mass but as the condition of belonging as such.

Agamben's version of co-belonging inverts the political imaginary of radicals from the sixties and seventies: many feared erasure, being commodified, being indistinguishable, being one of a mass. They rejected the terms of mass society and mass media, the forced collectivizing of their self-perception into the envelope of "us." Agamben accepts the mass without its collective form, thereby reformatting the momentary joy of dissolution into a whole as the singularity of belonging. Whatever beings do not shed or overcome their identities in an experience of massness. They already lack them. They can simply be as they are. The mass is the missing link – displaced mediator – the function of which is a chiasmatic inversion of properties. Baudrillard writes, "Banality, inertia, apoliticism used to be fascist; they are in the process of becoming revolutionary – without changing meaning, without ceasing to have meaning."[27] Baudrillard's warning to leftists in the seventies hits its target today: how is it that the evacuation of politics comes to embody the political as such?

Nevertheless, for Agamben the petty bourgeoisie displace or stand in for the mass, presenting thereby a new opportunity, an opportunity for a form of belonging unhindered by the division and specificity of "belonging to":

> Because if instead of continuing to search for a proper identity in the already improper and senseless form of individuality, humans were to succeed in belonging to this impropriety as such, in making of the proper being-thus not an identity and an individual property but a singularity without identity, a common and absolutely exposed singularity – if humans could, that is, not be-thus in this or that particular biography, but be only *the* thus, their singular exteriority and their face, then they would for the first time enter into a community without presuppositions and without subjects, into a communication with the incommunicable.[28]

We have been produced as subjects unlikely to coalesce, subjects resistant to solidarity and suspicious of collectivity. Central to this production is the cultivation and feeding of a sense of unique and special individuality. Every sperm is sacred: so began the story of our unique cellular lives. Or, every potential genetic combination carries with it the remarkable potentiality we locate in our individuated selves. Each voice must be heard (but they don't combine into a chorus). Each vote must be counted (but they add up to less than a movement). Each person must be visible (but then we don't see a group). Personalized "participatory" media is a problem not only because of its personalization of participation. More than that is its injunction that we participate ever more in personalization: make your own avatar, video, profile, blog, mobster, video, app. Participation becomes indistinguishable from personalization, the continued cultivation of one's person. Leave your mark.

What would happen if we just stopped? Agamben's evocation of singularity and belonging detached from a compulsion to cultivate an individual identity or to identify with a specific group opens up the potential for another form of belonging, one unlimited by the divisions and restrictions of being this or that. He suggests, moreover, that the beings who would so belong are not subjects in the sense that European philosophy or psychoanalysis might theorize. If some sort of identity served as a locus of ethical personality, and the search for this identity has been configured as an important ethical task (perhaps, as some philosophers would have it, the task of each human life), then whatever beings would emerge as those who are not subject to such tasks. Unburdened by the obligations of being this or that, of being bound by choices or words or expectations of meaning, whatever beings could flow into and through community without presuppositions.

Agamben asks what the politics of whatever singularity could be, what sort of politics could accompany "a being whose community is mediated not by any condition of belonging (being red, being Italian, being Communist) . . .but by belonging itself."²⁹ Because the course of his exposition of whatever being takes him through Saint Thomas Aquinas and limbo as the habitat of the souls of unbaptized children, the political question seems particularly vexing. Those in limbo lack God, but they don't suffer from this lack; they know nothing of it: "Neither blessed like the elected, nor hopeless like the damned, they are infused with a joy with no outlet."³⁰ With limbo long synonymous with a certain stuckness, with an in-between condition of persistence that is neither here nor there, with an inability to go forward or back, it is difficult to register a politics that we might admire or seek.

More specifically, I can locate here neither a politics I admire nor any sort of struggle at all. What could motivate whatever beings? What might move them? As Agamben conceives them, they seek nothing; they lack nothing. They co-belong without struggle or antagonism. It would seem, therefore, that they are not political beings at all; their being is a-political, beyond politics. They neither attack nor resist; they are neither inside nor outside. Perhaps it makes better sense, then, to think of the politics of whatever beings in terms of their setting. They are moved and propelled; they circuit through contemporary networks.

Souls in limbo belong in neither heaven nor hell. This condition of belonging to neither is also Agamben's model for a politics of absolute enmity toward the state. Agamben writes that "a being radically devoid of any representable identity would be absolutely irrelevant to the State."³¹ And so the state or, better, states would continue, unbothered and unlimited by the demands of people. States could attack and imprison, exploit and ignore – the future unfolding in and through militarized predatory robot drones. Whatever beings lack nothing and therefore demand nothing (and, presumably, they all get along just fine). No wonder they are irrelevant to the state. *The state can do what it wills. Whatever.*

For Agamben, however, rather than easing the way for unchecked state power, whatever being is the "principal enemy of the State." The state, he tells us, "cannot tolerate in any way . . . that the singularities form a community without affirming an identity, that humans co-belong without any representable condition of belonging."[32] Leaving to the side the question whether this intolerance is a property of the state or a more complex matter of a human subjectivity that is constitutively split, it seems clear enough that the state has from time to time tolerated and used the mass, a form of co-belonging without representable condition. The mass can threaten or support the state, can subvert or sustain it. In Baudrillard's conception, for example, the mass is neither a group-subject nor an object. On the one hand, the mass generally fails to become a conscious revolutionary force. On the other, it refuses attempts to make it speak. Surveys and statistics may simulate it, but the mass remains ungraspable, particularly as these very surveys are implicated in the reflexive constitution of the mass they survey. The absence of the mass, Baudrillard says, "is nevertheless intolerable."[33] It drives the repetitive processes of polling and testing. So not only can and has the state tolerated forms of co-belonging that do not affirm an identity, but the absence of an identity can itself generate processes of surveillance and incitement-to-speech useful for producing and maintaining power.

Agamben conceives the spectacle as language or communicativity. It is a form for the expropriation of linguistic being, a form that alienates people from language. He works here from the dilemma expressed by Debord: in the society of the spectacle, "the language of real communication has been lost" and a "new common language has yet to be found."[34] Debord writes: "Spectacular consumption preserves the old culture in congealed form, going so far as to recuperate and rediffuse even its negative manifestations; in this way, the spectacle's cultural sector gives over expression to what the spectacle is implicitly in its totality – *the communication of the incommunicable.*"[35] Agamben's response is to turn the problem into the solution and in so doing find in the spectacle "a positive possibility that can be used against it."[36] Communication of the incommunicable dissolves the gap between them. It tells us that even the incommunicable can be communicated, that it cannot be separated. Thus, the spectacle as the extreme expression of estrangement from linguistic being enables it own overcoming. The expropriation of language in the spectacle opens up a new experience of language and linguistic being: "not this or that content of language, but language *itself,* not this or that true proposition, but the very fact that one speaks."[37] Failure to communicate provides its own satisfaction, the enjoyment of language itself.

In the first chapter, I discuss Žižek's account of drive as loss: drive is loss as itself an object. Agamben's reflexive treatment of communication, his turn from *what* is said to *that* something is said, employs this logic of drive. Not only is a negative condition (estrangement from linguistic being) treated as a positive opening (new experience of belonging), but its positivity is a result of reflexivity. Language turns on *itself.*

Encountering again the reflexive logic of drive, we get a better sense of whatever being, of why it is the kind of being it is. Insofar as whatever beings experience their own linguistic being, they turn their attention from the content of language, from trying to communicate something, back to themselves as speaking. They shift from focusing on something outside or beyond themselves to turning back round upon themselves. In his discussion of the drive as precisely this turning round upon the self, Freud views it as a change from activity to passivity.[38] The active aim, to say something, is replaced by the passive aim, to have said. Whatever beings are passive, then, because they are subjects of drive. The very excesses of their communicative activity are the form of passivity.

Construing drive as a movement outward and back, Lacan employs the image of the headless subject. This acephalic subject of drive "has no relation to the subject other than one of topological community." Because drive involves but one surface or side of the subject, it isn't quite right to think of the "subject" of drive as actually a subject. Lacan says that "at this level, we are not even forced to take into account any subjectification of the subject."[39] We're considering a non-subjectivized subject, one characterized primarily by a lacuna; something is missing – the head! In fact, Lacan refers to the subject here as a lacunary apparatus, an apparatus that makes holes or that makes things turn up missing. The term "apparatus" suggests that this side of the subject, the side of the drive, is better conceived as an object. Lacan's term for this object that provides the other side or fundamental support for the subject is *objet petit a*, or loss itself as an object.

Whatever beings are set in the society of the spectacle, within the conditions of the alienation of language. They are effects of this expropriation of the commons, of a loss of meaning, difference, and individuality that turns this loss into their condition of belonging. Their setting is one of "the perfect exteriority that communicates only itself."[40] Their setting is the reflexive loop of drive.

9

To formalize the ways language provides a set of social links, Lacan presents formulas for four discourses, those of the Master, the hysteric, the university, and the analyst.[41] Each discourse takes its name from the figure that occupies the position of the agent that speaks in that discourse. Thus, the upper level of the discourse of the analyst is written $a - \$$ (*objet a* in the position of agent, subject-barred in the position of addressee). The lower level is written $S_2 - S_1$ (knowledge or the chain of signifiers in the position of truth and the Master signifier in the position of product or remainder). This lower level sits directly below the upper level such that a is written above S_2 and $\$$ is on top of S_1.

Žižek explains that in the discourse of the analyst, "the analyst stands for the paradox of the desubjectivized subject, of the subject who fully assumes what Lacan calls 'subjective destitution,' that is, who breaks out of the vicious cycle of the intersubjective dialectic of desire, and turns into an acephalous being of pure drive."[42] He concludes that the discourse of the analysis should therefore be correlated to radical-revolutionary emancipatory politics. Insofar as the analyst just sits there in the analytic situation, frustrating the poor subject by failing to provide it with a clear, symbolic place, the analyst is a part that is not a part of the situation (Žižek takes the term "part of no part" from Jacques Rancière). After all, that's why the analyst is paid – to function as an outside intrusion into the subject's life.

But what about a different reading of the formula of the analyst's discourse? Lacan notes that the analyst says to the subject, "Off you go, say everything that comes into your head, however divided it might be, no matter how clearly it demonstrates that either you are not thinking or else you are nothing at all, it may work, what you produce will always be admissible."[43] What if we insert this injunction to say whatever comes to mind in the blogipelago? What if we think of the social link of the discourse of the analyst as set within a declining symbolic order, an order which is barely ordered, where meaning slips and slides, getting momentarily stuck on nuggets of enjoyment?

If the discourse of the analysis is set within the decline of symbolic efficiency, then at least three things follow. First, the subject is desubjectivized or destitute. It is not structured in terms of symbolic identification so the analyst isn't functioning primarily as a marker of the gap in the symbolic – the instability of the symbolic has already been assumed, or the symbolic is so riddled with holes and gaps that they no longer appear as gaps of the Real (the Real cannot appear as such). Second, the object confronting and splitting the subject is itself a surplus enjoyment confronting and splitting the subject, threatening its fragile sense of itself – the stability of the Master is in the position of remainder. Third, we have entered the domain of drive, rather than desire. The analyst isn't only a figure of drive, then. The discourse as such persists in drive.

Set in drive, the formula for the discourse of the analyst can be read as a formula for whatever being. The *objet a* addresses a subject. It sends a message; it attempts to connect. Knowledge is in the position of truth (S_2 under the bar). But this knowledge is anything whatsoever; any sort of content or knowledge can support the agent/speaking object. Experience, mysticism, common sense, *my gut, my opinion* – in the absence of expertise, in the place of the decline of trust in so-called "expert" knowledge, I can use anything as a support for my view (fully aware that the fact that anything can be used actually means nothing can fully ground my position). This problem of any authority whatsoever appears in the formula: S_1, the Master, is below the bar, under the subject, in the position of production or remainder. Authority is remaindered, present but inoperative, unable to establish meaning.

In the setting of the decline of symbolic efficiency, the part of no part is not radical. It doesn't establish a break with the situation because there is not a situation that can be set or established as such. There is also no space for fantasy (the formula for fantasy does not appear). Whatever being doesn't allow for fantasy; it is premised on its foreclosure.

10

Contemporary networked media perform and repeat communicativity as such, the taking place of language. As applications for the expression of any idea whatsoever, of an opinion, such that it is, blogs continue the severing of expressions from their content and their authors. Ideas and opinions link together and circulate, expressions of themselves neither completely generic nor completely individual. Posts may link and gesture, but they don't represent themselves or anything else. They are expressions, such that they are. The measuring and counting, the hits and rankings, remind bloggers that we are set in intensive, reflexive, communication and entertainment networks. It's as if the compulsion to make the mass speak, to poll and survey it, now takes whatever being as its target. Blog stats don't track truth or meaning. They track blogging, the addition of posts, responses, and page views. Differently put, they track the fact of the spoken as they direct us away from what is said.

A better instance of language without referent, of language that refers only to the "it was said," is the word-cloud, a graphic representation of the content of a text understood in terms of frequency of word use. For example, a word-cloud made following the first debate between presidential candidates John McCain and Barack Obama during the 2008 election shows that McCain frequently used the words "know," "spending," and "got." Obama used the words "think," "make," and "going." He also used the word "got" with high frequency. We don't know what this means. But we do know that words were used and speeches were made. The irony here is that language as language itself, language reflected to itself as language – Agamben's ideal of the coming community – takes the spectacular form of the image.

In word-clouds, frequency and proximity displace meaning. Which words appear with which other words? The combination of these elements determines intensity – words that appear only once either don't count (they aren't counted) or they appear very faint and tiny, type as atmosphere. Words matter, not stories and not narratives. Words index communication – they mark that they are being communicated. Word-clouds shift away from a space of linguistically constituted meaning, away from a language constituted out of sentences that are uttered in contexts according to rules that can be discerned and contested.

What's lost? The ability to distinguish between contestatory and hegemonic speech. Irony. Tonality. Normativity – how can there be an ethics of the address if the words are not part of an address, if they are extracted from their position within speech acts to become artifacts and toys?. Critique. The terms prominent in a discourse can be discerned, but not what they mean, not even in relation to each other. We don't know the rules governing truth and falsity, which may suggest that there are no rules (other than those of frequency, proximity, and duration). Note that frequency can be citational or monological: that is, it can come from circulation or from self-repetition.

Message force multipliers are more important than the message. Word-clouds capture the shift from message to contribution characteristic of communicative capitalism.

The word-image of the word-cloud is prefigured in avant-garde art from the late nineteenth and early twentieth century. Cubists included words as images. Even more disruptive were the posters from Russian communist and Soviet revolutionary artists. On the one hand, their word-art was effective because of its revolutionary impulse, its challenge to the status quo of late Russian painting. It performed the revolution, disrupting prior meanings. On the other, precisely because it depended on its context for its performative efficacy, it reinforced the fact of symbolic meaning. Its disruption was not only to index language but to create a new one, to bring about a new world, a new man, a new register of meaning. The point wasn't to destroy meaning. It was to change it.

Word-clouds aren't revolutionary. They are elements of communicative capitalism, elements that reinforce the collapse of meaning and argument and thus hinder argument and opposition. Any words can be clouded. At Wordle you can make a new one out of speeches from Kennedy and Khrushchev, Ann Coulter or Sean "Puffy" Combs. Anyone you like.

The word-cloud image doesn't stand in for or provide a prosthetic word. It marks a feeling, an intensity. It doesn't ask that the viewer understand it. All the viewer is expected to do is register that the word has been, that it has appeared. The word become image is a feeling-impulse, like a badge. It's identificatory, relying on an identity between word and object. The word-image is this impulse-identity.

One can't argue with a word-cloud. It doesn't take a position. It marks a moment. It registers aspects of the intensity of that moment: repetition entails intensity, in this equation. But one doesn't know why or whether it's called for or what it's in relation to. It's just intense. The word-cloud might transmit the intensity, it might incite a feeling or a response, but it doesn't invite the interrogation of that response or what induced it. It offers representation without understanding: issues are out there. A word-cloud is like a Möbius strip where meta-data become noise: "she said a lot about politics and technology." Whatever.

4   Affective Networks

1

Why are blogs often portrayed as "inflicted" on the rest of us? Are the "rest of us," *everyone else in the entire world,* really *victims* of what is written on a single blog, in a single post, in a single thread? Or has the world somehow become the victim of bloggers, and not just of some specific blog, blogger, or group of bloggers, but bloggers in the abstract? What sort of world does this anxiety about bloggers presuppose or imagine?

The language of victimization in the face of bloggers inflicting their boring lives, their obsessive lives, their sex lives, their pets' lives on *the rest of us* differs from the criticism of rabid political bloggers or snarky celebrity bloggers all working 'round the clock to attack their specific targets and generally amplify and intensify the circuits of communicative capitalism. The difference is that the anxiety about victimization construes blogging per se as an activity that victimizes and harms regardless of any particular content. The practice of blogging itself is harmful. Harm is an embedded feature of the application, like a link or tag. Anxiety about blogging relies on an image of the world as a communicative one, a world wherein communication is ubiquitous and fragile, dangerous yet unavoidable. That bloggers are blogging is a fact of this world that one cannot escape.

The claim that blogging is harmful, that *the rest of us* are its victims, thus points to a crucial feature of blogging: it causes anxiety. Jacques Lacan associates the affect that is anxiety with *jouissance,* with the surplus enjoyment he designates as *objet a.*[1] Although anxiety seems to have no object (and thus differs from a fear or phobia), Lacan argues that it has to be approached in terms of *objet a*, in terms, that is, of surplus enjoyment. Anxiety about blogging, then, is anxiety about enjoyment.

In the preceding chapter, I present "whatever being" as a way to think about contemporary mediated subjects (although they can just as easily be designated as objects). In this chapter, I attend to the feedback loops, the circuits of drive, in which they are stuck. Without stable points of symbolic identification, whatever beings oscillate between the imaginary and the Real, crafting their ever-adaptable, morphing, identities even as they remain threatened and vulnerable to the success, presence, and enjoyment of others. Communicative capitalism commands us to enjoy, at the same time that it reminds us that we aren't enjoying enough, as much, or as well as others are. Our enjoyment remains fragile, risky.

Slavoj Žižek describes the way enjoyment constitutes itself as "stolen," or as present and possible only insofar as one is deprived of it.[2] *I would have read a serious novel, cultivated an organic garden, driven senior citizens to the polls if I hadn't gotten caught up in those stupid blogs. Why are all those people blogging, anyway? What makes their lives and experiences so much more interesting than mine?* If bloggers weren't inflicting their stupid stuff on the rest of us, the rest of us would be enjoying. We would be honing our writing, not reading the half-assed thoughts of idiots. We'd be making art, not looking at stupid cat videos. We'd be spending time with our family, not chatting with strangers on blogs. Blaming our failure to enjoy on bloggers thus compensates us for our failure by promising that *were it not for the bloggers* we would enjoy. Our failure, our insecurity, *is not our fault.* The language of infliction rests on the premise of fragile whatever beings threatened by the presence and enjoyment of others, preoccupied with the worry that others' lives are more meaningful and fun than their own. When they read our blogs and discover that our lives are really not worth the time it took to read about them, then they are furious, outraged – *why did you bloggers waste my time?*

The theft of enjoyment positions enjoyment as an object of desire. Allowing us to fantasize that we would actually prefer to be reading literary tomes, laboring in a weedy garden, and participating in a political process designed to ensure that political change never occurs, it postpones our confrontation with drive. Confident in what we would prefer to do, if only we could, we overlook what we are actually doing. *There's no way I spend three hours a day on Mafia Wars! It's* important *for me to tweet my reaction to the debate!* The fantasy of enjoyment covers over the fact that we are already enjoying, that we get off, just a little bit, in and through our multiple, repetitive, mediated interactions. Through that fantasy, we screen ourselves from the Real of our enjoyment, the enjoyment that we can't avoid, even if we don't want it.

Blog anxiety, then, expresses our anxiety in the face of our enjoyment. We are captured doing not what we want but what we must. The upshot is that we are more entrapped *after* the announcement of the death of blogging than we ever were while it ostensibly lived. Then blogging was an alternative. Now it's another unavoidable element of our ubiquitous media setting.

2

German media theorist Friedrich Kittler begins his influential book *Gramophone, Film, Typewriter* with optical fiber networks in order to get to an end: "Before the end, something is coming to an end."[3] The end, for Kittler, is in part an end of differentiation among forms of media storage and transmission; more specifically, the differentiation between image, text, and voice. Digitization brings this end about: "Instead of wiring people and technologies, absolute knowledge will be an endless loop."[4] I've been describing blogging's setting in communicative capitalism in terms of endless loops. Kittler's "absolute knowledge" coincides with our confrontation with an inability to know, our fundamental uncertainty regarding what is happening, will happen, and has happened, a confrontation we experience in and as capture in the repetitive circuits of drive.

A non-event on Christmas Day 2009 can illustrate the way abundant information degenerates possibilities for meaning. A Nigerian student, Umar Farouk Abdulmutallab, attempted to blow up Northwest Airlines Flight 253 over the city of Detroit. He was able to get past airport security by hiding the explosives in his underwear. Coverage of the failed bombing in the days after it didn't occur pointed out the numerous clues that should have alerted officials into preventing Abdulmutallab from boarding the plane. These included the fact that Abdulmutallab's father had notified the US Embassy in Nigeria that his son was missing and likely under "the influence of religious extremists based in Yemen," that he was listed in the "Terrorist Identities Datamart Environment," and that a communications intercept of Al-Qaeda followers in Yemen indicated that a man named "Umar Farouk" had volunteered for an operation.[5] Explanations for the security breach blamed "too much information" as well as an inability to access and analyze the information gathered. All the data in the world – as if such a fantasy of static completion were even possible – are useless without a question to cut through and organize them. Apparently, CIA computer systems "cannot easily search automatically – and repeatedly – for possible links." According to the Chair of the House Science and Technology Committee's Investigation and Oversight Subcommittee, "Railhead," a program supposed to provide the National Counterterrorism Center with an integrated information infrastructure, is plagued by so many design errors that not only does it fail to connect the dots, "it can't find the dots."[6]

To return to Kittler: he treats the distinctions between image, text, and voice in terms of the Lacanian registers of the imaginary, Symbolic, and Real. Lacan's registers, he tells us, are in fact an historical effect of changes in storage technologies. The imaginary consists in the cuts and illusions that comprise fantasies of wholeness, be they fantasies incited before a mirror or on the screen. The Symbolic is typing, the machinic word in all its technicity. The Real is recorded sound, inclusive of the hisses and noise accompanying the vocals produced by a larynx. Digitization erases the distinctions between visual, written, and acoustic media. It turns all data into numbers that can be stored, transmitted, copied, computed, and rearranged. Taking the place of the material differences providing the basic structure of Lacanian psychoanalysis is the feedback loop. Kittler writes, "A simple feedback loop – and information machines bypass humans, their so-called inventors. Computers themselves become subjects."[7] The codes and computations of machinic circuits thus herald an end, the end of "so-called man."

Contra Kittler, we're not there yet – and it doesn't look like we'll get there from here. The affective networks of communicative capitalism indicate that machines are not terminating humans. On the contrary, cybernetic circuits don't exclude humans – they connect them (computers don't need emoticons to help them access the feeling of a message). It's almost as if Kittler remains more of a humanist than he wants to admit: his technology cryptograms, surface-wave filters, computational devices, and fiber-optic cables rest on an underlying fantasy *if only there were a human element.*

The snares of communicative capitalism persist in and deploy human intensities, all the way to the inhuman dimension of the drives. As Žižek writes, "We become 'human' when we get caught into a closed, self-propelling loop of repeating the same gesture and finding satisfaction in it."[8] People *enjoy* the circulation of affect that presents itself as contemporary communication. The system is intense; it draws us in. Even when we think we aren't enjoying, we enjoy (*all this email, I am so busy, so important; my time is too precious to waste on another Facebook game . . . but my score is going up; it's such a burden having so many, many friends – oh, and I should tweet about it so they know how busy I am*).

Blogs, social networks, Twitter, YouTube: they produce and circulate affect as a binding technique. Affect, or *jouissance* in Lacanian terms, is what accrues from reflexive communication, from communication for its own sake, from the endless circular movement of commenting, adding notes and links, bringing in new friends and followers, layering and interconnecting myriad communications platforms and devices. Every little tweet or comment, every forwarded image or petition, accrues a tiny affective nugget, a little surplus enjoyment, a smidgen of attention that attaches to it, making it stand out from the larger flow before it blends back in. We might find ourselves more fearful or seem somehow secure, even if we have no idea what we're looking for or what we've found. Unable to find a given dot, we feel, in ways that exceed our conscious perception, the movement of multiple colliding dots.

These affective links are stronger than hypertextual ones. Their resonance remains and continues after specific links are no longer operative. In flame wars, spam, and critical linking (linking not as a sign of affiliation but as evidence of something awful, outrageous, to-be-combated), intense feeling accompanies and reinforces code. Even failures to forward and refusals to link have affective impact: *Why didn't she friend me? Why didn't he put me on his blogroll?* In a world of code, gaps and omissions can become knots of anxiety.

Affective attachments to media are not in themselves sufficient to produce actual communities – bloggers are blogging but the blogosphere doesn't exist. Neither does the circulation of affect through multiple, networked media imply stimulus junkies in blank-eyed isolation before their screens. Affective networks produce feelings of community, or what we might call "community without community." They enable mediated relationships that take a variety of changing, uncertain, and interconnected forms as they feed back each upon the other in ways we can never fully account for or predict. So while relations in affective networks merge and diverge in ways resistant to formalization, the circulation of intensities leaves traces we might mark and follow: blog anxiety, mood flows on Twitter, military message intensification, irrational exuberance.

3

2009 was the year of Twitter. Even before the so-called "Twitter Revolution" in Iran ("so-called" because US preoccupation with tweets occluded the more mundane organizing done with paper and pencil), Twitter's 140-character updates were widely heralded as the next phase of social media, for better or worse. With Twitter, one can send and receive messages to one's network ("followers") from either laptop or phone, thereby staying in touch with a group while away from the computer. Twittering – like updates on Facebook – lets users keep connected without having to trouble with sending or responding to individual text messages. Users don't even need to concern themselves with specific followers. They can find and follow updates by topic, a practice enabled by hashtags, or phrases preceded by the hash sign (the number or pound sign). Rather than keeping abreast of what Joe is doing, for example, I can track tweets on specific issues.

By 2009, politicians and celebrities seemed to be tweeting their every move (some US members of Congress tweeted during President Barack Obama's first State of the Union address). Their tweets were archived and circulated, perpetual reminders of the inanity of these momentary updates. Large websites and blogs began to feature twitter rooms, pages of twittered posts grouped thematically by poster (journalist, celebrity, right-wing political operative). Non-politicians and non-celebrities also tweeted. Even when our tweets weren't followed by more than a couple of hundred people, it still felt like something to issue updates and statements.

Not surprisingly, commentary was mixed. For Alexander Zaitchik, Twitter feeds a growing "constant-contact media addiction, birdlike attention-span compression, and vapidity to the point of depravity." What happens when the communication standard is 140 characters? What comes next? "Seventy characters? Twenty? The disappearance of words altogether, replaced by smiley-face and cranky-crab emoticons?"[9] *Wired*'s Clive Thompson is more enthusiastic, in a "bright side of crack" sort of way. An early adopter, Thompson was already celebrating the "stupefyingly trivial" aspect of Twitter in the summer of 2007.[10] For him, multiple, mindless updates result in something more, a kind of ambient awareness or "social proprioception." They have a cumulative effect, producing a sense of others' everyday lives and feelings.

Lauren Berlant describes Facebook's news feed:

Facebook is about calibrating the difficulty of knowing the importance of the ordinary event. People are trying there to eventalize the mood, the inclination, the thing that just happened – the episodic nature of existence. So and so is in a mood right now. So and so likes this kind of thing right now; and just went here and there. This is how they felt about it. It's not in the idiom of the great encounter or the great passion, it's the lightness and play of the poke.[11]

Like a tweet, a Facebook update marks the mundane by expressing it, by breaking it out of one flow of experience and introducing it into another. Now part of a shifting screen of comments and images, the mundane moment tags a mood or sensibility. Differently put, because updates are aspects of a practice, singular moments among many such moments, they both contribute to an affective flow and mark divergences from it. Little moment-to-moment reports suggest the pattern of changes in one's feelings about one's life, what is worth noting and why. The flow is the result of these multiple offerings, back and forth, up and down, on and on. The feel of the updates arises out of their setting, a setting that is a little different for everyone – not all your friends are mine. The fact of uttering, of adding in, displaces the content of any one utterance. The flow of tweets transmits what exceeds any specific tweet: that is, a broader, less tangible, more general mood. One even gets accustomed to overlooking tweets in their singularity, enjoying instead getting swept into their flow.

By the summer of 2009, a study of 11.5 million Twitter accounts showed that the ambient awareness of Twitter was heavily tilted toward a small number of super users and a bunch of automated zombies.[12] Just 5 percent of the accounts were generating 75 percent of the tweets – another example of power laws on the web (the authors of the report refer to Twitter's "hockey-stick-like growth").[13] Likewise, while about 1 percent of users tweeted ten or more times a day, over 85 percent tweeted less than once a day (and half hadn't updated in over a week) – a finding hardly suggestive of an environment where one starts to sense the rhythms and feelings of the lives of others . . . unless, of course, the others in one's environment are marketers, advertisers, and automated bots. We were sensing not just networked generated moods, not just the multiplication of the feedback effects of our tweets, but the directed channeling and amplification of some streams over and against others. The Sysomos study found that 24 percent of the tweets were coming from automated bots, feeds from elsewhere on the net, like Second Life (2,000-plus updates per day from this virtual world) or Dogbook (Facebook for dogs). It also determined that "social media marketers are far more active than overall users."[14] Perhaps #Twitter tags the reflexivity of contemporary media networks as they turn back upon themselves.

4

One of the numerous scandals extending out of and around George W. Bush's aggressive war against Iraq involved the Pentagon's organization of former generals as media talking heads. Not only did these "military analysts" advocate war, parroting administration talking points, but many were also tied to the defense industry as executives, consultants, and board members.[15] According to the *New York Times*, "Internal Pentagon documents repeatedly refer to the military analysts as 'message force multipliers' or 'surrogates' who could be counted on to deliver administration 'themes and messages' to millions of Americans 'in the form of their own opinions.' "[16] The term "message force multipliers" suggests one of the ways that state political power operates under communicative capitalism.

I say "suggests" because the term "message force multipliers" can be accented in at least two ways: the force multiplication of messages or the multiplication of message forces. Force multiplication indexes a communications strategy for a complex media environment. It implies adding lots of forces, putting more people on the ground or on the air, just as one would send more troops into a situation. It's like spam for television – which is not the same as propaganda. The term "propaganda" isn't useful in an age of constant media, ever-present advertising, unavoidable spin. The government's provision of forces differs from spam on the internet, though, because it's spam by request – television news shows invite the military analysts to appear and analyze what's going on. In this way, the mainstream, commercial media (including large right-wing blogs) *ask* to be bearers of the administration's media. They set themselves up to be its tools, its voice – when they aren't, they lose what they understand as access to power, to "the story." News, then, is what the administration reports, and the mainstream media are the neutral vehicle – medium – for it (as if they had no responsibility for the practice formerly known as "journalism"). In psychoanalytic terms, this instrumental relation is perverse. Media position themselves as the means for others' enjoyment, whether that enjoyment is the administration's or, more likely, their sponsors'.

"Multiplication of message forces" indicates a concrete awareness of the affective dimension of media in communicative capitalism. The Bush administration excelled in excepting itself from the signifying aspect of language and relying instead on affective prompts. It absorbed the lesson from advertising and pop music: repetition exerts a force, a compulsion; repetition has effects independent of the meaning of what is repeated. Repetition itself has an affective impact – a sexualizing pulsation, a threatening intrusion, a hilarious extreme. State politics in the twenty-first century in the US, UK, and Europe has become ever more adept at tying together previously stable meanings in ways that rely on and at the same time disrupt these meanings. This combination of reliance and disruption generates affective responses from the tension accompanying the combustion of meaning and non-meaning.

The combination also suggests a tactical appreciation for contemporary short attention spans. With multiple message forces, one can keep a message alive on one terrain even as it dwindles in another – a role at which blogs excel. Issues that seem to have died can reanimate: mainstream journalists report, "bloggers are debating . . ." or "as was recently uncovered by blog X. . . ." The idea of multiplying message forces highlights how messages carry affective charges. The communications strategy on which it is based doesn't turn on "getting our message out there," as if there were to be a debate on positions that need to be understood and considered. Rather, the goal is spreading, diversifying, and intensifying the message force. Abundant, dispersed, mashed-up messages thus displace previous communication strategies focused on direct image control. Even when facts are corrected, fictions remain, repeated and circulated in affective networks. The generals were vehicles for this spreading and distributing – message force genbots.

My account here shares elements of Tiziana Terranova's description of informational culture. She writes, "an informational culture marks the point where meaningful experiences are under siege, continuously undermined by a proliferation of signs that have no reference, only statistical patterns of frequency, redundancy and resonance (the obsessive frequency and redundancy of an advertising campaign, the mutually reinforcing resonance of self-help manuals and expert advice, the incessant bombardment of signifying influences)."[17] Such a media environment could be read in information theory's oppositional categories of signal and noise. This reading would indicate that the way to get one's message across would be to eliminate noise and establish a clear channel of communication (perhaps by "going over the heads" of the media and "speaking directly to the people"). Terranova rightly eschews the binary of signal and noise, arguing instead for the turbulent materiality of communication wherein information as such relies on "distracted perception." For example, architecture and design induce bodily habits directly implicated in the processing of information. Signal and noise, then, not only exert reciprocal effects on each other but contribute to feedback processes in the environments out of and through which they are generated, transmitted, and received.

Terranova's discussion is persuasive and surely right: information is more than the delivery of a coded signal. Yet her jump to the active, material, dimensions of information relies on two omissions. The first is the split within a message between its content and the fact of its being sent, what I call its "contribution" (and what Lacanian psychoanalysis treats in terms of the enunciated and the enunciation).[18] The recipient of a message can ask, "What does this mean?," attending thereby to a message's content. She can also ask, "Why are you sending me this?," drawing out the deliverer's purpose or intent, what the deliverer aims to contribute by sending the message. Terranova, explicating key debates in information theory, omits this doubling of the utterance into content and contribution, noting that communication at its most minimal depends on the establishment of a clear channel. For information theorists such as Claude E. Shannon, it simply doesn't matter who is sending and receiving.

Terranova's omission, while responsive to information theory, occludes a key feature of networked communication: the displacement of content by contribution – more specifically, by communication for its own sake. Contemporary affective networks rely on the marking, adding, forwarding, and circulating of messages not because doing so "means" something but simply to communicate. As with Cicero's *causerie*, described in chapter 2, contemporary communication is whatever communication, the communication of communicativity. Tweets, Facebook updates, images of cute kitties, text messages – these media of affective flow can be limited neither to their content nor to their materiality. Understanding them requires attending to their doubling as message and contribution and grappling with the ways that the latter's displacement of the former amplifies the chaotic, intensive, circulation of enjoyment even as it diminishes the impact of any single contribution.

The second omission effected by Terranova's jump to a materiality rendered as chairs and keyboards, bottles and telephones is its neglect of the materiality already at play in perceiving. Perception as such is "distracted," contorted around a stain or gap. As I discuss in chapter 2, one of the ways Lacanian psychoanalysis theorizes this gap is in terms of the gaze. This concept designates the way that one's perceptions are always partial and incomplete. As we fill them in, we infuse our perceptions with inadequacies and distortions.[19] For example, the subject might fill in what he wants to see; his desire may fill in the gaps he encounters. He may then become aware of such a gap, and his involvement in it, turning his attention from the object of perception to himself as perceiver. The point is that perceiving requires attending to some aspects of a setting rather than others, even as that attending may be involuntary, compelled by an element in a situation, unconscious, or a deliberate effort at focusing one's attention on one's breath rather than on the multiple stresses of one's day.

As a tactic in the Bush administration's communications strategy, message force multipliers presuppose both the displacement of content by contributions and distracted perception. They thrive, in other words, not in a closed media environment but in the open, distributed, recombinant, chaotic feedback loops of affective networks. In contrast to a state politics waged through message force multipliers, Terranova claims that opinion polls, surveys, and risk assessments are "the most effective and concise modality of information transmission today."[20] Her response is to advocate a "cultural politics of information."

One component of a cultural politics of information would posit "radically other codes and channels." Although the very notion of "radically other" makes it impossible to imagine or assess such codes and channels (if they could be imagined or assessed, they wouldn't be "radically" other but would be in some relation to our current setting; likewise, insofar as they are "radically other," their political implications are unknowable), Terranova's suggestion could be valuable. Yet her analysis is premised on a too quick mapping of information theory onto information politics. Under communicative capitalism, an excess of polls, surveys, and assessments circulates, undercutting not only the efficacy of any particular poll or survey but the conditions of possibility for knowledge and credibility as such. There is always another survey, done by another group or association with whatever bias and whatever methodology, displacing whatever information one thought one had.

Another component of Terranova's cultural politics of information would pursue digitalizing tendencies to decompose and recombine, tendencies she associates with montage (via the work of Pierre Lévy). Given Lacan's association of montage with the drive and the repetitive jumping among heterogeneous elements, decomposition and recombination appear more as aspects of our capture in affective networks than as tactics of resistance. Differently put, drive as montage indicates how media tactics of resistance such as mash-ups and remixes are already captured: not only do they contribute to the ever-circulating flow, amplifying the intensity of the very elements they seek critically to recombine, but in presuming the efficacy of a politics of meaning they displace attention from the fact that the multiple elements of our contemporary media ecology are already fragments and parts ready for recombination.

The politics that montage suggests is a politics released from burdens of coherence and consistency. It needs neither theme nor message but can employ questions and repetitions. It is not a politics that relies on "the intensity of the image and the afterlife that such intensities carry" but one that has already challenged and undercut, remastered, recontextualized, and mashed-up innumerable uploaded and recirculated images.[21] Understood in terms of drive, montage clicks on a politics that exceeds the constraints of narrative, appearing as a combination of disparate images shifting and mutating without beginning or end, head or tail. In the setting of communicative capitalism, we might also think of such a politics in terms of links and windows, text messages and blog posts, contributions to the flows into which any addition is absorbed. What's clear is that far from a left-wing political application, montage is well suited to a political Right, in both its neoliberal and its neoconservative guise, insofar as this Right thrives on uncertainty, insecurity, and turbulence as easing the flow of affective intensities and consolidating our capture in the networks of drive.

5

More than a decade before his famous recantation of the ideology that had guided his life (and brought global financial markets to their knees), Alan Greenspan, then chair of the US Federal Reserve Board, gave a speech at the American Enterprise Institute where he was being honored with a prestigious award. Entitled "The Challenge of Central Banking in a Democratic Society," the speech outlined the history of the Federal Reserve, particularly with regard to maintaining the purchasing power of money. Greenspan pointed out the difficulties with inflation and unemployment in the 1970s, crediting a turn away from Keynesianism and toward monetarism as key to remedying those economic problems. Yet he also confronted an emerging non-knowledge or loss in knowledge at the level of the economy.

Greenspan noted the complexity of "pinning down the notion of what constitutes a stable general price level." If prices are necessary for measuring inflation, which prices matter? Do escalating stock and real estate prices pose a problem to economic stability? What about "the price of a unit of software or a legal opinion"? The combination of informatization and the post-industrial shift toward the service sector's increased role in the economy eluded the standard mechanisms for assessing changes in prices and hence inflation.

Technology figures heavily in Greenspan's speech. The Chairman mentioned costly equipment expenditures associated with increasing the safety and reliability of electronic payments: "like a breakdown in an electric power grid, small mishaps create large problems." As if foreshadowing the economic débâcle that would cascade from the collapse of the investment banking firm Lehman Brothers twelve years later, Greenspan observed as well the risks associated with financial interconnectivity, "the failure of a single institution will ricochet around the world, shutting down much of the world's payments system."

Most of the press on his speech, though, highlighted his gesture to the booming stock market (the Dow Jones Industrial Average had risen nearly 3,000 points over the preceding two years), a rise seemingly driven by internet stocks, despite the fact that no information technologies were yet included in the Dow: "how do we know when irrational exuberance has unduly escalated asset values?"[22]

The dotcom bubble didn't burst for four more years. It intensified and expanded. Not only did the Dow rise another 5,000 points, but stocks, markets, and investing infused US popular culture, becoming intense attractors of interest and attention. For some, including Greenspan, the key factor behind the market boom was the fact that the country had entered into a "new era." Technology and competition created new opportunities for prosperity and growth – indeed, whole new ways of conceptualizing prosperity and growth. For others, that increases in corporate earnings in the mid-nineties coincided with popular uptake of the internet (the Mosaic browser was released in 1994; the internet backbone was fully pushed into the private sector by 1995) did not mean that computers and the internet themselves caused the increases.[23] Most of the internet companies – despite their extraordinarily successful initial public stock offerings – were not themselves making a profit.

Still, the internet *felt* profitable. It felt new, exciting, innovative. Greenspan emphasized "awesome changes."[24] Net cheerleaders like *Wired* editor Kevin Kelly celebrated the expansion in opportunities ushered in by the net, an expansion so significant that firms could stop thinking in traditional economic terms like productivity and problem-solving. More important were conversations, relationships, networks, all of which amplified value (even if this value couldn't be quantified or monetized). Kelly thus emphasized ever-extending feedback loops: "each actualization of an idea supplies room for more technology, and each new technology supplies room for more ideas. They feed on each other, rounding faster and faster."[25]

Critics, also identifying the internet with feedback loops, saw the booming stock market not as proof of a new economic era but of a speculative bubble with its own self-fulfilling momentum. Where Kelly perceived "opportunity cascades," economist Robert Shiller saw "information cascades": that is, people – investors – taking a kind of information short-cut by assuming that what everyone else is doing must be right.[26] For example, if we believe our friends are on Facebook, we will join. Even if our friends aren't there yet, after we've joined, they will, too. During the dotcom bubble of the nineties, herd behavior, copying the actions of others, started to make sense – in fact, not doing so when all these others seemed to be becoming millionaires felt irrational, like being left behind, a dupe and a sucker.

Applying George Soros's theory of reflexivity in financial markets (described in chapter 1), John Cassidy argues that the reflexive process of the nineties bubble was most powerful in the technology sector.[27] The same technology on which people were speculating was enabling ever more speculation. America Online, CompuServe and E*Trade allowed independent investors to trade online (by 1999 over five million US households had online trading accounts).[28] Likewise, computer-linked day traders (there were over sixty day trading firms in 1999) quickly bought and sold stocks as they tried to profit from small shifts in price.[29] Both groups relied not only on networked trading but also on the ever-increasing deluge of financial information – cable news, financial chat rooms, close to real-time share prices. Exchanges of tips and opinions amplified both the popular feeling that money was being made and the individual sense that one had the information necessary to join right in. Using internet technologies to make money seemed to prove that the technologies themselves were money-makers, money-makers without limit, even when, especially when, the actual companies showed no profits and quickly burnt through their venture capital. Some of the more spectacular collapses included Pets.com (which lost over $100 million) and eToys (with debts over $270 million).

The rapid, expanding, intensifying circulation of information and capital traced a loop around a change in knowledge. Not only did the speculative bubble indicate that markets could be irrational, that prices could well be the outcome of irrational exuberance, and that people would speculate on the fact that predicting exactly when the bubble would burst was impossible, but the information superhighway didn't seem to provide much information. The issue is not the typical lament regarding search engines and filters. It's the fact of fundamental non-knowledge and uncertainty. Even *Wired* editor and network propagandist Kevin Kelly acknowledges this point as he urges his readers to jump, act, risk, move – anything can be an opportunity; one doesn't know what will work, what will fail. Tucked at the very end of his *New Rules for the New Economy* is Kelly's version of the decline of symbolic efficiency: "Because the nature of the network economy seeds disequilibrium, fragmentation, uncertainty, churn, and relativism, the anchors of meaning and value are in short supply. We are simply unable to deal with questions that cannot be answered by means of technology."[30]

A decade after the dotcom bust, the so-called "advanced" economies confronted the even more extreme and devastating collapse of the credit, mortgage, and finance markets, again in the wake of a massive bubble of irrational exuberance. Investors had convinced themselves that they had the mathematical formulae and computing skills necessary to shield themselves from risk, neglecting the fact that "when enough people subscribe to a particular means of taming financial risks, then that itself brings new risk."[31] Barely three months before the collapse of Lehman Brothers ushered in a "once in a century" financial and economic calamity, another *Wired* editor embraced and exaggerated Kelly's point about our inability to deal with questions that can't be answered through technology. Chris Anderson pronounced that such questions need not even be asked – the "data deluge" makes science and theory obsolete: "This is a world where massive amounts of data and applied mathematics replace every other tool that might be brought to bear. Out with every theory of human behavior, from linguistics to sociology. Forget taxonomy, ontology, and psychology."[32] Neglecting the ways human behavior leads not just to bubbles but to the rational irrationality of short-term investments precisely because everyone else is doing it contributes mightily to extreme fluctuations in financial markets, at great human cost (estimates of the loss of wealth in the 2008–9 crisis exceed ten trillion dollars). Anderson similarly ignores how interpretations of data both shape data and are themselves also data. Differently put, he omits the fact that interpretations of behavior influence behavior. This neglect of feedback is particularly shocking coming from an editor of *Wired*.

6

In his *Comments on the Society of the Spectacle*, published twenty years after *The Society of the Spectacle*, Guy Debord offers the notion of the "integrated spectacle" as the highest stage of the

spectacular society. Although he doesn't describe the integrated spectacle as a reflexive circuit or as the spectacle's
turning in upon itself, such reflexivity seems to be its primary
conceptual innovation. Debord writes, "For the final sense of
the integrated spectacle is this – that it has integrated itself
into reality to the same extent as it was describing it, and that
it was reconstructing it as it was describing it. As a result, this
reality no longer confronts the integrated spectacle as something alien."[33] The integrated spectacle is an element of the
world it depicts; it is part of the scene upon which it looks. It
is a circuit.

Debord misses the circuitry of the integrated spectacle
because his account of the spectacle is embedded in a model
of broadcast media. His arguments thus proceed as if the
problem of the spectacle remained, for all its dispersion, ultimately a matter of top-down control, of actors and spectators.
Debord worries about images as the individual's "principal
connection to the world." The problem, though, isn't with the
image's displacement of language and critical thought or even
with its commodity-function. Rather, Debord's worry stems
from the fact that the images the spectator sees are "chosen
and constructed by *someone else.*"[34] When "chosen by someone
else" is the problem, the solution seems like it can be found
in choosing and constructing for oneself – *and maybe with cool
Free Software, or with photo and video uploading and sharing
capabilities: freedom through Apple and Flickr.* If the problem of
the image is that it comes from "someone else," then participatory technology is the solution. Anyone who makes her own
images is a threat, a radical, a revolutionary. But this solution
leaves out underlying questions of access and ownership, not
to mention the fundamental trap of an ever-intensifying image
environment as more and more of us upload videos to
YouTube. Debord suggests that in the spectacular society,
"those who control information" can alter at will individual
reputations. He doesn't consider what changes when we alter
our images ourselves (*I should have never posted those party pics
on Facebook!*). He can't allow, in other words, for the possibility
that in choosing for ourselves, in participating in the production of the spectacle, we might contribute to our own capture.

Discussion poses a problem similar to the manipulated image. Debord claims that "spectacular discourse leaves no room for any reply."[35] This doesn't apply to contemporary networked information and entertainment media: it's easy to "reply all" – although these replies, like the others circulating around and through us, don't feel like responses; they are just more contributions to be deleted, stored, or forwarded. Debord writes that people have "never been less entitled to make their opinions heard."[36] Again, under communicative capitalism, the opposite is the case. Everyone not only has a right to express an opinion, but each is positively enjoined to – *vote, text, comment, share, blog*. Constant communication is an obligation. Every interaction, transaction, inaction, reaction is construed in terms of a conversation. Debord rightly emphasizes the repetition constitutive of the spectacle. Arguments in the spectacle prove themselves "by going round in circles," "by coming back to the start." Yet he laments that "there is no place left where people can discuss the realities which concern them."[37] Today people discuss the realities that concern them everywhere and all the time – blogs, Facebook, Twitter, they ooze with the realities of individual concern. Talk. Talk. Talk. Discussion, far from displaced, has itself become a barrier against acts as action is perpetually postponed. What appears as an exchange of reasons is a vehicle for the circulation of affects. The lack of action is the abundance of discussion viewed from a different angle.

Debord criticizes the experts who serve the media and state, experts he presents as falsifiers and fools. His argument, again reinforcing an underlying assumption that participatory media technologies might prove a way out of spectacular society, relies on a faith in amateurs, in ordinary people, individuals with the "capacity to see things for themselves."[38] Insofar as Debord's critique positions professionals as completely bound to the spectacular state, it relies on a suspicion toward expertise. Not only can expert knowledge not be trusted, but there is really no such thing as expertise: "the ability to falsify is unlimited."[39] Failing to follow his argument to the end, Debord implies that non-expert knowledge necessarily brings with it capacities for resistance and transgression. This may be true under mass media, particularly in the case of censorious mass media. In the setting of communicative capitalism, another name for the impossibility of expertise, for falsification without limit, is the decline of symbolic efficiency. How do we know whom to believe or trust? Suspicion or even uncertainty toward expertise goes all the way down: skepticism toward politicians and the media, scientists and academics, extends to local knowledges, knowledges rooted in experience, and anything at all appearing on the internet. Not only has amateurism and gut-level or street knowledge supplanted what was previously considered expertise, but even amateur and everyday knowledge is now rejected as nothing more than opinion, and opinion which is necessarily limited, biased, and countered by others. The ability to falsify *is* unlimited. The lack of a capacity to know is the other side of the abundance of knowledge.

Finally, correlative to the embeddedness of Debord's critique of the image, discussion, and expertise in mass media is his presumption that the spectacle is a form of state power, that it is a vehicle for mastery over the people. Understood reflexively, constant, pervasive communication can be a regime of control in which the people willingly and happily report on their views and activities and stalk their friends. Networked whatever beings don't need spectacles staged by politicians and the mass media. We can make and be our own spectacles – and this is much more entertaining. There is always something new on the internet. Corporate and state power need not go to the expense and trouble to keep people entertained, passive, and diverted. We prefer to do that ourselves. Mark Andrejevic's analysis of the constellation of voyeurism and self-disclosure in interactive media (his focus is on the reality television message boards Television Without Pity) persuasively demonstrates the ways even dismissive, critical engagement with television binds viewers more closely to the shows they claim to hate. The result, he argues, is a "reflexive redoubling that amounts to an active form of self-submission."[40] Networked, participatory spectacles let us stage and perform our own entrapment.

Debord provides a helpful list of the features of society at the stage of the integrated spectacle:

1   Incessant technological renewal (which surrenders every-
    one to the mercy of specialists).
2   Integration of state and economy.
3   Generalized secrecy.
4   Unanswerable lies (have eliminated public opinion which
    has lost the ability to make itself heard).
5   An eternal present.[41]

I offer the following alterations as a way of upgrading Debord
for communicative capitalism:

1   Incessant technological renewal (which contributes to the
    production of amateurs and a sense that no specialist ever
    really knows).
2   Neoliberalization of governance (the state uses it power to
    maintain inequality, supporting the privilege of financial
    elites; Debord's account remains bound to a critique of
    technocracy and the welfare state).
3   Generalized publicity (revelation and disconcealment: for
    example, the US government can admit to torture and face
    no significant repercussions).
4   A decreasing ability to distinguish between truth and lies,
    a decline of a politics where truth matters (collapse of
    symbolic efficiency).
5   A focus on what's next, prediction, forecasting, the biggest
    thing after the next biggest thing.

Debord's claim that, in the society of the spectacle, "the uses
of media guarantee a kind of eternity of noisy insignificance"
applies better to communicative capitalism as a disintegrated,
networked, spectacular circuit.[42] Key to this circulation is the
fact that networks are not only networks of computers, proto-
cological and fiber-optic networks. They are also affective networks capturing people.

If we revisit the discussion of Agamben from the preceding
chapter, we recall that the spectacle returns us to our linguistic
nature in an inverted fashion. The spectacle contains and captures the possibility of a common good. We could even say its
production of a common is its good or that the power of spec-

tacle is its production of the common as a feeling, necessarily shared. Its form is inseparable from its affect. A spectacle is affective form and this is its common good.

7

Critical media theorists have recently begun to consider the affective dimension of networks. Describing the shift in thought toward affect, Patricia Clough writes that the "affective turn" marks "an intensification of self-reflexivity (processes turning back on themselves to act on themselves) in information/communications systems, including the human body; in archiving machines, including all forms of media technologies and human memory; in capital flows, including the circulation of value through human labor and technology; and in biopolitical networks of disciplining, surveillance, and control."[43] Some of the recent work on affect and media technologies extends out of Michael Hardt's and Antonio Negri's *Empire* (which is influenced by Gilles Deleuze and Félix Guattari). In the context of outlining Empire as a new global political-economic formation, Hardt and Negri discuss the expansion and proliferation of communication networks as well as the role of informatization in the post-Fordist economy. Among the changes in labor they associate with informatization is "the production and manipulation of affect."[44] Here they are concerned with feelings – of attachment, affection, excitement, fear, ease, or well-being – as products. Hardt and Negri view affective labor as including such seemingly diverse sectors as entertainment, health care, and women's unpaid labor. Each of these areas involves the production of feelings, be they those of thrill and amusement, vitality and security, or care and belonging. Women's affective labor is particularly important to Hardt and Negri's account because it produces social networks. They don't link these social networks directly to the internet, however, nor do they take up the disruptive dimensions of networked intensities. Nonetheless, their association of affective labor with the production of social networks opens up the possibility of conceiving communication networks not simply in terms of linked machines but as networks that are constitutively affective.

Alexander Galloway and Eugene Thacker go further in this direction as they critique Hardt and Negri for relying on a simple symmetry between Empire and the revolutionary force opposing it, the multitude. For Galloway and Thacker, the network form itself needs to be interrogated, particularly with regard to the constitutive tension "between unitary aggregation and anonymous distribution, between the intentionality and agency of individuals and groups on the one hand, and the uncanny, unhuman intentionality of the network as an 'abstract' whole."[45] My claim is that this uncanny intentionality is best understood via the psychoanalytic notion of drive. The loops and repetitions of the acephalous circuit of drive describe the movement of the networks of communicative capitalism, the ways its flows capture subjects, intensities, and aspirations. Accompanying each repetition, each loop or reversal, is a little nugget of enjoyment. We contribute to the networks as creative producers and vulnerable consumers because we enjoy it. In fact, the open architecture of the internet enables and requires the capture of enjoyment insofar as it is premised on users' contributions, alterations, and engagement. It's not like cinema, where people only have to show up. For the internet to function at all (as is abundantly clear in Web 2.0 and 3G mobile networks), people have to use it, add to it, extend it, play with it. Our participation does not subvert communicative capitalism. It drives it. Again, contemporary information and communication networks are essentially affective networks.

Terranova also jumps off from Hardt and Negri's discussion of Empire in terms of a network of networks. Particularly compelling in this regard is her rejection of all too-static accounts of the internet as a global grid or extended database that displace attention from movement in and through the networks. Communication networks are dynamic. Terranova writes, "A piece of information spreading throughout the open space of the network is not only a vector in search of a target, it is also a potential transformation of the space crossed that always leaves something behind – a new idea, a new affect

(even an annoyance), a modification of the overall topology."⁴⁶
This something left behind, this product of movement through
the networks, should be thought in terms of enjoyment: both
result from circulation through a communicative space.

Terranova approaches this affective production, however,
via the image (she positions the image as a sort of bioweapon
in an informational ecology). Although the image is too restric-
tive a notion to account for the variety of contributions to
contemporary networks – music, sounds, words, sentences,
games, videos, fragments of code, viruses, bots, crawlers, and
the flow of interactions themselves as in blogs, Twitter,
Facebook, and YouTube – Terranova rightly highlights that
what's at stake in the image "is the kind of affect that it packs,
the movements that it receives, inhibits, and/or transmits."⁴⁷
The most interesting aspect of the image, in other words, is
the way that it is not simply itself but itself plus a nugget or
shadow or trace of intensity. An image is itself and more.

Psychoanalysis can be of some assistance in theorizing the
movements Terranova associates with affect. As Joan Copjec
points out, both Freud and Lacan associate affect with move-
ment.⁴⁸ Freud viewed affect as a kind of displacement, representation's fundamental "out-of-phaseness" with itself. The
conventional view of the displacement of affect treats it as the
distortion of perception by an excess of feeling. Copjec dis-
agrees, arguing that the affective experience of something as
moving indexes a movement beyond the perceiving individual,
a surfeit or excess that ruptures the perception, making it
more than itself and enabling it to open up another register
(for Lacan, the Real; for Deleuze, the virtual). Affect, then,
is this movement, a movement which estranges the subject
from its experience. A thought, memory, or perception is
affective to the extent that it opens up or indexes something
beyond me.

I can't help but think of the cute cat photos and funny
animal videos that circulate on the net. Why do people upload,
forward, and link to these? It's not only because cats are cute
or even because one's own cat is completely interesting. It's
that the feeling that the cuteness accesses, the feeling that
moves it, opens to something more, to a kind of beyond or

potential. The dimension of affect is this "more than a feeling" that imparts movement. The potential here may be for connection (though one should be careful not to reduce affect to the intentions of the subject sending cute cat photos), but not necessarily – anyone who uses email knows how annoying forwarded cuteness can actually be. Cute sayings or images are also not the only contributions that circulate: funny videos, shocking statements, pressing opportunities, silly applications all inhabit contemporary communication networks. They all provide momentary, even fleeting, charges and intensities, interruptions and divergences.

Insofar as affect as a movement designates a doubling of an image, utterance, perception, or sound into itself and something else, we can account for the affective discharge of reflexivized communication. The additive dimension of communication for its own sake designates an excess. This excess isn't a new meaning or perspective. It doesn't refer to a new content. It is rather the intensity accrued from the repetition, the excitement or thrill of more. In the reflexive doubling of communication, the enjoyment attached to communication for its own sake displaces intention, content, and meaning. The something extra in repetition is enjoyment, the enjoyment that is captured in the drive and the enjoyment that communicative capitalism expropriates.

At the same time that affect is movement, there is a specific affect that is a halting or arrest. Copjec invokes the image of running in place. This affect that is an inhibition of movement is anxiety. The experience of anxiety is a confrontation with excessive enjoyment: one encounters what is in one more than oneself, an alien yet intimate kernel at the core of one's being. Copjec writes, "*Jouissance* makes me me, while preventing me from knowing who I am."[49] Finding oneself face-to-face with *jouissance*, one is pulled between incomprehensibility and extreme intimacy.

Copjec identifies two versions of the experience of anxiety: exposure to the excess of our unrealized past and to the punishing, relentless super-ego, itself an altered form of *jouissance* (as Žižek frequently puts it, the fundamental injunction of the super-ego is Enjoy!).[50] In the first instance, my anxiety results from encountering past alternatives: *What would I have become had I stayed in that relationship? What would have happened had I arrived the next day instead?* Copjec writes, "For, in the experience of anxiety, one has a sense not only of being chained to an enjoyment that outstrips and precedes one, but also of the opacity of this enjoyment, its incomprehensibility and unassumability, which is dependent, I have argued, on its being grounded in nothing actual, in a 'thrust-aside' past that never took place."[51] Facing my enjoyment, uniquely mine but alien and seemingly unchosen, I cannot avoid the unsettling question "how did I get here?"[52]

We should also add to this aspect of anxiety the enjoyment of the other. As Žižek explains, one of the ways that the subject organizes enjoyment is via fantasies about the other. These fantasies express essential features of our own enjoyment. For example, homophobic treatments of gay men as excessively promiscuous, as having frequent, intense, anonymous sexual encounters, express the homophobe's suppositions regarding real sexual satisfaction (consequently, for conservatives, gay marriage threatens marriage itself by eliminating its supplemental fantasy: that one sacrificed real sexual satisfaction for its sake; this sacrifice is necessary for the sacred character of marriage – without it, sex becomes common, conventional, and rather boring; in other words, the worst that the homophobe can imagine is that gay sex is just as boring as married sex). Žižek writes: "the fascinating image of the Other gives a body to our own innermost split, to what is 'in us more than ourselves'; and thus prevents us from achieving full identity with ourselves. *The hatred of the Other is the hatred of our own excess of enjoyment.*"[53]

In the second instance, the experience of anxiety results from the super-ego injunction to enjoy. The super-ego commands the subject to an impossible enjoyment, to find complete fulfillment in sex, exercise, professional achievement, a fabulous vacation. The very impossibility of fulfilling this injunction not only suffocates the poor subject but also incites a flight away from anxiety and toward the pursuit of knowledge.[54] To avoid the anxiety of the *jouissance* that prevents me from knowing who I am, I come under a compulsion to "Keep on knowing more and more," a compulsion or thrust that Lacan associates with an "epistemological drive."[55] The attempt to escape anxiety thus results in capture at another level. Lacan associates this capture with science, capitalism, and the discourse of the university. We can extend this point by noting their contemporary merger and materialization in networked information and communications media (after all, the internet arose in the context of government-sponsored research, initially carried out not only at the Department of Defense but also at a small number of universities, the linking together of which provided the groundwork for the internet that was later opened up to commercial interests and celebrated as the primary figure of global capitalism).

To reiterate, the object of anxiety is surplus *jouissance*, designated by Lacan as *objet petit a*. Copjec presents it in terms of a confrontation with an unrealized past as well as with the super-ego, a confrontation the subject attempts to flee by pursuing knowledge. Her account of anxiety corresponds to what Žižek (following Jacques-Alain Miller) designates as "constitutive anxiety": that is, "confrontation with *objet petit a* as constituted in its very loss," that is, *objet petit a* as an object of drive.[56] In both instances, the object is loss (rather than lost): the loss of an unknowable past (rather than a specific experience), the loss of a capacity to obey or comply (no matter what one does, one cannot satisfy the super-ego). The blockage or stuckness of anxiety, then, is at the same time the repetitive, circular movement of drive, the force of loss.

The point becomes clearer when we consider epistemological drive: keep on knowing more and more. In Lacan's account in Seminar XVII, this "keeping on" results from the change in the status of the Master in university discourse: that is to say, a change in the status and function of knowledge. Because university discourse cannot be anchored, cannot be held in place by an ultimate truth or injunction, it keeps on keeping on knowing. It doesn't come to an end or reach an ultimate goal. It circulates, and its circulation is an effect of its failure to anchor. Nothing can stop the progress of science; nothing can stop the movement of ideas. Information wants to be free – to circulate round and round. The more knowledge we accrue, the less we know. Abundance from one perspective is lack from another.

The networks of communicative capitalism are affective because they are characterized by drive. Their affective dimension thus should not be reduced to desiring productivity or a nurturing emotional practice. *Contra* Hardt and Negri, networked communication is better understood via the negativity of drive, a negativity that results in stuckness and movement, rupture and creativity, a negativity, in other words, capable of accounting for the reflexivity in real networks (so, negativity here connotes positive feedback and the excess of an effect in relation to its cause). More crudely put, the affective charges we transmit and confront reinforce and extend affective networks without encouraging – and, indeed, by displacing – their consolidation into organized political networks.[57] While this circulation might constitute a kind of affective labor, it is affective labor that is already captured.

In fact, rather than presuming the fit of the category of labor, we do better to note the persistent disagreement among bloggers and net researchers regarding work and play in social networks. When we blog, are we working or playing? If we are working, then for whom are we working? Who enjoys or who accrues enjoyment? If we enjoy, does that mean we are actually playing?[58] Or might the instability here index the fact that we are caught in circuits of drive wherein we cannot escape enjoyment but neither can we assume or accept it as our own?

Lost horizon/loss as horizon

The now old cyberpunk fiction of a cyberspace, techno-utopian fantasy of an information frontier, and still lingering supposition of "the Internet" as a domain separate from "real life" continue to dwindle as imaginaries of an outside. Global communications networks connect through a variety of devices, technologies, and media – internet, mobile phones, radio, television, global positioning systems, game platforms, etc. One of the more interesting features of massive multiplayer online role-playing games is the intersecting of game and non-game worlds: players can buy and trade currencies and characters outside the gamespace. What initially appears as the most separate and complete realm for living fantasies quickly opens up into the actualities of financial markets, wage labor, and exploitation. The expansions and intensifications of networked interactions thus point not to a closed field but to the non-all Real of human interaction.

In his later work, Žižek supplements the "Lacanian account of the Real as that which 'always returns to its place' – as that which remains the same in all possible (symbolic) universes."[59] He adds the notion of a parallax Real: that is, a Real capable of accounting for the multiplicity of appearances of the same underlying Real. Such a parallax Real is a gap or shift between perspectives. It does not embody a substantial point of information or sensory perception (*you feel it in your gut; I feel it in my bones*). Rather, it is the shift from one perspective to another. The Real, then, does not refer to what is the same but to the "hard bone of contention which pulverizes the sameness into the multitude of appearances." It is retroactively posited as the necessary yet impossible cause of this very multiplicity. In other words, the parallax Real denotes multiplicity and its impossible core, a "purely virtual, actually nonexistent X."[60]

Such a notion of a parallax Real is well-suited to communicative capitalism. What appears is multiplicity, pulverization, the constant and repeated assertion of something else, something different. To the extent that the shifts of perspective appear immediately (without interpretation, meaning, elevation to the status of a universal), they obscure the fact of contention, as if the shifts were among a multitude of singularities each with its own perspective, none of which is more powerful, more structural, or more true than another (an example from the US is the way that conservatives accuse liberals of racism when liberals argue for racial diversity in political appointments). What is obscured is the underlying gap or disavowal, the virtual X of fundamental antagonism. The multiplicity of shifts effaces their embeddedness in capitalism – more specifically, the communicative capitalism that makes their expression possible. If the Real is ultimately impossible, then it names the obstacle we come up against in our supposition and experience of reality. In communicative capitalism, that obstacle is the (missing) efficiency of the symbolic.

The Real of the internet is the circulatory movement of drive – the repeated making, uploading, sampling, and decomposition occurring as movement on the internet doubles itself, becoming itself *and* its record or trace – effected by symbolic efficiency as loss. The movement from link to link, the forwarding and storing and commenting, the contributing without expectation of response but in hope of further movement (why else count page views?) is circulation for its own sake. Drive's circulation forms a loop. The empty space within it, then, is not the result of the loss of something that was there before and now is missing. The drive of the internet is not around the missing Master signifier (which is foreclosed rather than missing). Instead, it is the inside of the loop, the space of nothing that the loop makes appear. This endless loop that persists for its own sake is the difference that makes a difference between so-called "old" and "new" media. Old media sought to deliver messages. New media just circulate.

Understanding this circulation via drive enables us to grasp how we are captured in its loop, how the loop ensnares. First, we enjoy failure. Insofar as the aim of the drive is not to reach its goal but to enjoy, we enjoy our endless circulation, our repetitive loop. We cannot know certainly; we cannot know adequately.[61] But we can mobilize this loss, googling, checking Wikipedia, mistrusting it immediately, losing track of what we are doing, going somewhere else. We are captured because we enjoy. This idea appears in writing that associates new media with drugs, "users" and "using," as well as colloquial expressions like "Facecrack." (As a friend said to me, well, why didn't you tell me Mafia Wars is like crack? Now I'll totally play!) Thomas Elsaesser illustrates the point via YouTube. Describing his movement among the links and videos, he writes,

after an hour or so, one realizes on what fine a line one has to balance to keep one's sanity, between the joy of discovering the unexpected, the marvelous and occasionally even the miraculous, and the rapid descent into an equally palpable anxiety, staring into

the void of a sheer bottomless amount of videos, with their proliferation of images, their banality or obscenity in sounds and
commentary.[62]

Failure, or what Elsaesser tags "constructive instability," is
functional for communicative capitalism; it's our ensnare-
ment in the loop of drive.

Second, we are captured in our passivity or, more precisely,
by the reversion of our active engagements and interventions
into passive forms of "being made aware" or "having been
stated." The problem, then, is that ubiquitous, personal media,
communication for its own sake, turn our activity into passivity. They capture it, use it. We end up oscillating between
extremes. On the one hand, we have opinions, theories, ideas,
and information that we want to share. So we write our books
and blogs, adding in our contribution to the circulating flow.
Just what was needed – another blog. On the other hand, the
information age is an age wherein we lack the information we
need to act. As communicative capitalism incites a continuous
search for information, it renders information perpetually out
of reach. Outraged, engaged, desperate to do *something*, we
look for evidence, ask questions, and make demands, again
contributing to the circuits of drive. A concrete example here
is the George W. Bush administration's torture policy. Before
and after Bush left office, a refrain circulated concerning the
need to get to the truth of the situation, to see more photographs, to read more documents – as if it had not been known
since at least 2004 that the US was torturing prisoners captured in the so-called "war on terror." Since photographs and
documents already were circulating, since members of the
Bush administration – including Vice President Cheney – had
already acknowledged that they did in fact approve the policy
of torture, the problem was not the absence of information.
What was missing is instead more radical: namely, a capacity
to see ourselves as acting rather than querying, searching,
waiting for action to happen.

Christian Marazzi makes a related observation in his
description of imitative behavior among those working in the
finance sector. He writes, "One important result of the empiri-

cal studies of the behavioral finance theorists is this very notion of *imitative behavior* based on the *structural information deficits* of all investors, be they large or small. . . . The modalities of communication of what the 'others' consider a good stock to invest in counts more than what is communicated."[63] Psychoanalysis associates an imitative, competitive relation to others with imaginary identification. Imitative behavior can thus be read as an index of the decline of symbolic efficiency. Unable to find a standpoint from which to assess the adequacy of the available information, bond traders and hedge fund managers mimic those around them, creating cascades and bubbles.

The gaze (discussed in chapter 2) draws us to a third way we are captured in contemporary communication networks. Because the gaps are not filled (because perception as such is distorted), because they cannot be filled, we are drawn to them, inscribing ourselves in the images we see, the texts that we read. So although online interactions like blogging might initially appear as so many ways that we search for ourselves, trying to know who we are, to pull together our fragmented identities, the other aspect of the gaze, its traumatic disruption of the image, is perhaps even more crucial. Lacking answers, ever more uncertain, we become mesmerized by our own looking, entranced by the reversal of looking for an object to looking at ourselves as objects, to becoming objects ourselves. I can approach the same idea from a different direction: the satisfaction provided by identifying with a group also arises from transgressing the group's expectations. Scary zombie pop-ups spliced into conventional YouTube videos illustrate this point. Just as the viewer has become absorbed in the video, perhaps searching for the ghost or the key to the magic trick, a monstrous image accompanied by a hideous scream shocks her out of her absorption, reminding her that, in a way, the fault is hers – she shouldn't have been wasting her time watching videos online, shouldn't have let her guard down, shouldn't have presumed that the video images had a flow independent of her investment in them.

Contemporary communication networks are reflexive: we, the users, are creating them. We are producing the environment we inhabit, the connections that configure us. We provide the feedback that amplifies or ignores (or write the code that provides the feedback that amplifies or ignores). We are configuring the worlds we inhabit, yet they are ever less what we desire but haven't reached and ever more what we cannot escape yet still enjoy. I have argued throughout this book that the psychoanalytic concept of drive helps explain our current media trap. As it designates the plasticity of the objects to which we become attached, the repetitive movements of our attachment through networks, and the extremes and disequilibria inextricable from the circuits that result, drive indexes the primary structure of enjoyment for contemporary whatever beings.

Affective networks capture users in circuits of drive. The more we contribute, the more extensive our submission. More bluntly put, as we share our opinions and upload our videos, there are more opinions to read and videos to watch and then more responses to craft and elements to mash up. And then there are still more responses to read, and as these increase so do the challenges of finding the ones we want. At that point, we can see what the crowd thinks, what has passed muster, risen to the top, been shared, forwarded, and recommended. The result looks like a power law distribution (like any hit movie, song, or best-selling novel) – new voices are disadvantaged, those without language, media, and visual skills will remain lost in the flow.

With each click and intervention, moreover, we make a mark that can be traced, capitalized, and sold. This does not mean that systems of surveillance and expropriation are seamless and efficient. On the contrary, intensifications can disrupt, overload, and crash particular sites and servers. They can register as new trending topics on Twitter and in the blogipelago, perhaps even getting a minute or two of airtime on cable news and maybe occasioning a piece in one of the few remaining print magazines or newspapers (as if these were properly political ends). The displacement of political conflict to the terrain of networked media has the perverse repercussion of perpetually expanding the topography of struggle even as it constantly signals the locations, intentions, and networks of those who are fighting. This expansion has thus far strengthened communicative capitalism as it feeds on accelerating crises and emergencies. It also increases the exposure and vulnerability of those engaged in active protest and resistance on the ground. No wonder the diversion of cute cat photos is so welcome.

Some readers will no doubt disagree with me. They will want to emphasize all sorts of tools and apps that enable activists to coordinate and get their messages "out there," as if media politics today were a politics of messages rather than one set in the decline of symbolic efficiency. Most likely, they will point enthusiastically to sites like MoveOn (a US-based site that coordinates fund-raising, petition, letter, and fax-campaigns for liberal and left causes) and underplay the far right and white supremacist message boards.[64] They may extend the heroic, outsider ethic of the hacker into the practices of bloggers, as if the setting and subjectivities had remained the same, as if the last decades of networked media had not configured the users.

Other readers will assume I'm a luddite or technophobe and thereby avoid taking up the harder task of thinking through the disadvantages, costs, and challenges the turbulent media environment poses for an anti-capitalist politics oriented toward economic and social equality. It's easier to set up a new blog than it is to undertake the ground-level organizational work of building alternatives. It's also difficult to think through the ways our practices and activities are producing new subjectivities, subjectivities that may well be more accustomed to quick satisfaction and bits of enjoyment than to planning, discipline, sacrifice, and delay, subjectivities that may well eschew equality as an end.

Most readers will likely find my analysis here too bleak, despite the fact that I said from the outset that critical media theory should forswear affective offerings of hope and reassurance. These readers will emphasize contingency and the unexpected. After all, we can't predict the future; it's an open field of potentialities (I think tendencies are stronger in some directions than they are in others). The question, then, is whether a media politics that does not merely circulate contributions is possible or if a politics capable of overturning communicative capitalism must emerge via a cut through the circuits of drive. The former course of media politics ranges from the cultivation of critical media competencies and local, face-to-face, street-level activism to the organization of covert cells of communist hackers. Each of these attends to practices of subjectification that might work against the limbo of whatever being. The latter course of the cut through drive also needs the skills of the communist hackers and the local ties of street activists, although it could result from completely unpredictable crises or from the amplification of the effects of predictable disturbances cascading through complex networks. So even if the revolutionary overthrow of communicative capitalism seems like the remnant of twentieth-century fantasies (although it shouldn't), the reality of extremes, turbulence, and destruction in the reflexive circuits of complex networks cannot be avoided. It can at best be channeled, reinforced, and retroactively determined in directions less likely to exploit and immiserate. Both courses, alternative media politics and the cut through drive, need critical media theory. But neither should presume it's sufficient: as long as politics is reduced to communication, it will remain captured.

Notes

Chapter 1   Blog Settings

1   As the contributions to *New Media: 1740–1915*, edited by Lisa Gitelman and Geoffrey B. Pingree (Cambridge, MA: MIT Press, 2003), exhaustively demonstrate, media – and notions of mediation – have histories; technologies that now seem quaint were once new media.

2   For a thoughtful meditation on time and media, see Siegfried Zielinski, *Deep Time of the Media*, translated by Gloria Custance (Cambridge, MA: MIT Press, 2006).

3   For a discussion of communicative capitalism, see my *Publicity's Secret: How Technoculture Capitalizes on Democracy* (Ithaca, NY: Cornell University Press, 2002) and *Democracy and Other Neoliberal Fantasies* (Durham, NC: Duke University Press, 2009).

4   Theodor Adorno, *The Culture Industry* (London: Routledge, 1991) 84.

5   See Jonathan Beller's analysis of efforts to capitalize the attention economy with respect to Google, *The Cinematic Mode of Production: Attention Economy and the Society of the Spectacle* (Hanover, NH: Dartmouth College Press, 2006) 302–8.

6   Michael Hardt and Antonio Negri, *Empire* (Cambridge, MA: Harvard University Press, 2000). See also my discussion of their account of informatization and the postmodernization of the economy, "The Networked Empire," in *Empire's New Clothes: Reading Hardt and Negri*, edited by Paul A. Passavant and Jodi Dean (New York: Routledge, 2004) 265–88.

7   David Harvey, *A Brief History of Neoliberalism* (New York: Oxford University Press, 2005) 3.

8   "Pwnd," pronounced to rhyme with "owned," is a term from the world of online gaming that means that one has been

defeated, dominated, or disgraced. I am indebted to my son, Kian, for his knowledge of the term's use, pronunciation, and proper spelling (other spellings indicate that the user is a "noob").

9 See the Anarchopedia entry on the GNAA, http://eng. anarchopedia.org/Gay_Nigger_Association_of_America (accessed March 22, 2010).

10 In the best book on surveillance and new media to date, Mark Andrejevic puts the concept to excellent use; see *iSpy: Surveillance and Power in the Interactive Era* (Lawrence: University Press of Kansas, 2007) 251–4. Wendy Hui Kyong Chun, *Control and Freedom: Power and Paranoia in the Age of Fiber Optics* (Cambridge, MA: MIT Press, 2006), also draws from Žižek's notion of the decline of symbolic efficiency (269–71). Chun wrongly suggests that Žižek believes that "reasserting symbolic paternal authority will reinforce symbolic authority," thereby missing entirely the point of his discussion of the death(s) of the father(s) in *The Ticklish Subject* (London: Verso, 1999).

11 Slavoj Žižek, *The Plague of Fantasies* (London: Verso, 1997) 150–3.

12 Dany-Robert Dufour has a similar discussion in *The Art of Shrinking Heads*, translated by David Macey (Cambridge, UK: Polity, 2008).

13 *Plague* 150.

14 *Plague* 163.

15 Žižek writes, "In short, the properly dialectical paradox resides in the fact that *the very 'empirical', explicit realization of a principle undermines its reign*"; *The Indivisible Remainder* (London: Verso, 1996) 195.

16 *Plague* 155.

17 *Indivisible Remainder* 196.

18 *Indivisible Remainder* 196.

19 *Plague* 156.

20 My reading of Žižek's account of the loss of the Real of the Other, over-proximity, and paranoia corrects some of the errors in Chun's treatment of paranoia in *Control and Freedom*. Missing the way that the function of the signifier is always virtual, Chun asks whether "being a father" can "stand as a primordial signifier now that fatherhood can be scientifically determined" (271).

The problem here is twofold. First, the symbolic function of the paternal signifier had nothing to do with the "being" of a father. There was always a necessary gap between being and signification ("standing"). Lacan explains in Seminar XVII: "The real father is nothing other than an effect of language and has no other real . . . the notion of the real father is scientifically unsustainable"; Jacques Lacan, *The Seminar of Jacques Lacan, Book XVII: The Other Side of Psychoanalysis*, edited by Jacques-Alain Miller, translated by Russell Grigg (New York: W.W. Norton, 2007) 127. Second, that the function of the paternal signifier is in decline, that it has changed fundamentally as a result of universalized reflexivity, is precisely Žižek's point (*Ticklish Subject* 342–7).

Additionally, insofar as she fails to understand that the changes in communicative capitalism fundamentally impact the very possibility of meaning, Chun mistakenly presents paranoia in terms of "inadequate information" and "technologies' vulnerabilities" (267–8). In connection with her assertion that the problem of paranoia involves ignoring "the difference between possibility and probability," these remarks obfuscate what's at stake in the decline of symbolic efficiency, namely, the conditions of possibility of adequation and credibility (259). No amount of information, technology, or surveillance will compensate for the change in the symbolic.

In the terms of the early Lacan to whose analyses of psychosis Chun refers, the foreclosure of the paternal signifier means that there is nothing that can hold together the chain of significations (although there are possibilities for momentary stabilizations of meaning/significance effected through *objet petit a*). The change in the symbolic is Real. As Žižek writes, "The suspension of the function of the (symbolic) Master is the crucial feature of the Real whose contours loom on the horizon of the cyberspace universe" (*Plague* 154). For the subject, the consequence of this absence of symbolic mediation of the imaginary and the Real is suffocating closure before the intrusions of the unbearable *jouissance* of the other. Chun's appeal to a view of freedom as vulnerability thus remains trapped in the terms that she endeavors to critique: the vulnerable subject threatened by the *jouissance* of the other is strictly correlative to the decline of the symbolic and the absence (and resulting overproximity) of the other *qua* Real.

21   *Indivisible Remainder* 190.
22   Ulrich Beck, *Risk Society: Towards a New Modernity*, translated by Mark Rittter (London: Sage Publications, 1992).

23   See also Andrejevic's discussion of terrorism and reflexivity in *iSpy*, 163–86.

24   Richard Gray, "Legal Bid to Stop CERN Atom Smasher from 'Destroying the World'," *Telegraph* (August 30, 2008). Available at http://www.telegraph.co.uk/news/worldnews/europe/2650665/Legal-bid-to-stop-CERN-atom-smasher-from-destroying-the-world.html (accessed March 22, 2010).

25   Dennis Overbye, "Gauging a Collider's Odds of Creating a Black Hole," *New York Times* (April 15, 2008). Available at http://www.nytimes.com/2008/04/15/science/15risk.html (accessed March 22, 2010).

26   *Ticklish Subject* 336.

27   Mark C. Taylor, *Confidence Games: Money and Markets in a World without Redemption* (Chicago: University of Chicago Press, 2004) 285.

28   Beck 171.

29   Although beyond the scope of my discussion here, I should note the centrality of reflexivity to the sociology of Pierre Bourdieu. See Pierre Bourdieu and Loïc Wacquant, *An Invitation to Reflexive Sociology* (Chicago: University of Chicago Press, 1992).

30   Quoted in Paul Mason, *Meltdown: The End of the Age of Greed* (London: Verso, 2009).

31   Ulrich Beck, *World Risk Society* (Cambridge, UK: Polity, 1999) 111.

32   For example, see George Soros, *The Crash of 2008 and What it Means* (New York: Public Affairs, 2009).

33   Nassim Nicholas Taleb, *The Black Swan: The Impact of the Highly Improbable* (New York: Random House, 2007) xxii.

34   See also Clay Shirky, "Power Laws, Weblogs, and Inequality" (February 8, 2003). Available at http://www.shirky.com/writings/powerlaw_weblog.html (accessed March 26, 2010).

35   *Publicity's Secret*.

36   An excellent analysis of this migration (via the interdisciplinary Macey Conferences) comes from N. Katherine Hayles, *How We Became Posthuman* (Chicago: University of Chicago Press, 1999).

37   Steven Johnson, *Emergence: The Connected Lives of Ants, Brains, Cities, and Software* (New York: Scribner, 2001) 143.

38   Johnson 151.

39   Johnson 206.

40 Tiziana Terranova, *Network Culture: Politics for the Information Age* (New York: Pluto Press, 2005) 122.

41 Terranova 122.

42 Michel Foucault, *The Birth of Biopolitics: Lectures at the College de France, 1978–1979*, translated by Graham Burchell (New York: Palgrave Macmillan, 2008) 159–60.

43 Fred Turner, *From Counterculture to Cyberculture* (Chicago: University of Chicago Press, 2006) 35–6.

44 Turner 240.

45 Turner 244.

46 Turner 245.

47 Turner 219.

48 Turner 194.

49 Christopher M. Kelty, *Two Bits* (Durham, NC: Duke University Press, 2008) 2.

50 Kelty 58.

51 See Albert-László Barabási, *Linked* (New York: Plume, 2003).

52 Kelty 309.

53 Kelty 7.

54 Jürgen Habermas, *The Structural Transformation of the Public Sphere*, translated by Thomas Burger (Cambridge, MA: MIT Press, 1989) 28.

55 Reinhart Koselleck, *Critique and Crisis* (Cambridge, MA: MIT Press, 1988) 82.

56 This is a highly condensed version of an argument I make in *Publicity's Secret*, chapter 1.

57 Kelty 51, 308.

58 Fredric Jameson, "The Vanishing Mediator: Narrative Structure in Max Weber," *New German Critique* 1 (Winter 1973) 52–89; 78.

59 Slavoj Žižek, *Tarrying with the Negative* (Durham, NC: Duke University Press, 1993) 228.

60 The url for the now suspended project is: http://www.deadmedia.org/ (accessed March 22, 2010). See also Henry Jenkins, *Convergence Culture* (New York: New York University Press, 2006) 13.

61 Jacques Lacan, *The Seminar of Jacques Lacan, Book VII: The Ethics of Psychoanalysis*, edited by Jacques-Alain Miller, translated by Dennis Porter (New York: W.W. Norton, 1992) 212. See also Paolo Virno, "General Intellect," translated by Arianna Bove. Available at http://www.generation-online.org/p/fpvirno10.htm (accessed March 22, 2010).

62 *Seminar VII* 212.

63   Slavoj Žižek, *The Parallax View* (Cambridge, MA: MIT Press, 2006) 63.

Chapter 2   The Death of Blogging

1   Hugh Mcleod, "Why We're All Blogging Less," posted August 12, 2007. Available at http://gapingvoid.com/2007/08/12/why-were-all-blogging-less/ (accessed March 23, 2010).

2   The notion of blogipelago is informed by Albert-László Barabási's work on directedness in complex networks, *Linked* (New York: Plume, 2003), as well as by Chris Anderson's notion of the long tail, *The Long Tail* (New York: Hyperion, 2006).

3   Mark Day, "Blogs Still Rule, Despite the Dictatorship of Idiots," *The Australian* (March 29, 2007) 18.

4   "User-Generated Content Uncovered," Brand Republic, posted August 25, 2006. Available at http://www.brandrepublic.com/bulletins/digital/article/589413/usergenerated-content-uncovered-power-people/ (accessed March 23, 2010).

5   See the *Business Week* cover story, "Blogs Will Change Your Business," May 2, 2005.

6   "2009 State of the Blogosphere: The Full Blogworld Presentation," Michael Arrington, posted at TechCrunch, October 16, 2009. Available at http://www.techcrunch.com/2009/10/16/2009-state-of-the-blogosphere-the-full-blogworld-presentation/ (accessed March 23, 2010). Thanks to Geert Lovink for the link.

7   "McDonald's Fake Lincolnfry Blog," posted at Strategic Public Relations, February 6, 2005. Available at http://prblog.typepad.com/strategic_public_relation/2005/02/mcdonalds_fake_.html (accessed March 23, 2010).

8   Charles C. Mann, "Spam+Blogs=Trouble," *Wired* 14.09 (September 2006). Available at http://www.wired.com/wired/archive/14.09/splogs.html (accessed March 26, 2010).

9   See Dave Sifry, "The State of the Live Web, April 2007," posted April 5, 2007. Available at http://www.sifry.com/alerts/archives/000493.html (accessed March 23, 2010).

10   Jay David Bolter and Richard Grusin emphasize the difference between immediacy and hypermediacy in *Remediation: Understanding New Media* (Cambridge, MA: MIT Press, 1999).

They write, "If the logic of immediacy leads one either to erase or render automatic the act of representation, the logic of hyper-mediacy acknowledges multiple acts of representation and makes them visible" (34–5). Crucial to their distinction is their critical perspective on immediacy as falsely naturalizing: that is, as pretending an illusory access to an unmediated reality. I am less interested in terminology here than I am in the instability of the distinction in the context of user-generated content and the massification of interpersonal media devices: media (our absorption in a media environment, our impulses to mediate our experiences) are immediate.

11 "2009 State of the Blogosphere" (see note 6 above).

12 Posted by Tim at the blog "Road to Surfdom," May 9, 2006. Available at http://www.roadtosurfdom.com/2006/05/09/blog-whining-fatigue/.

13 See *International Blogging*, edited by Adrienne Russell and Nabil Echchaibi (New York: Peter Lang Publishing, 2009).

14 "Far East Leads the World for Web Users Reading and Writing Blogs," *New Media Age* (July 9, 2007) 13.

15 See Sifry.

16 Quoted from London's the *Sunday Times* by Day.

17 Mark Andrejevic provides an excellence account of surveillance in *iSpy: Surveillance and Power in the Interactive Era* (Lawrence: University Press of Kansas, 2007).

18 The distinction between desire and drive here comes from Slavoj Žižek's psychoanalytic (Lacanian) Marxism. He takes up the distinctions between these economies of enjoyment in various places, including *The Parallax View* (Cambridge, MA: MIT Press, 2006). For a summary see Jodi Dean, *Žižek's Politics* (New York: Routledge, 2006).

19 Jacques Lacan, *The Seminar of Jacques Lacan, Book XI: The Four Fundamental Concepts of Psychoanalysis*, edited by Jacques-Alain Miller, translated by Alan Sheridan (New York: W.W. Norton, 1981) 177.

20 Slavoj Žižek, *The Ticklish Subject* (London: Verso, 1999) 297.

21 *Ticklish Subject* 297.

22 For a history, see Rebecca Blood, "Weblogs: A History and Perspective," posted at Rebecca's Pocket, September 7, 2000. Available at http://www.rebeccablood.net/essays/weblog_history.html (accessed March 23, 2010). Geert Lovink, *Zero Comments: Blogging and Critical Internet Culture* (New York: Routledge, 2008) 5.

23   Meg Hourihan, "What We're Doing When We Blog," posted at O'Reilly Web DevCenter, June 13, 2002. Available at http://www.oreillynet.com/pub/a/javascript/2002/06/13/megnut.html (accessed March 23, 2010).

24   Anne Helmond examines the ways that the close association between blogs and search engines affected blogging as a practice; "Blogging for Engines," MA Thesis, Media Studies, University of Amsterdam, submitted January 28, 2007.

25   For a discussion of the fantasy of abundance on the internet, see Jodi Dean, "Communicative Capitalism: Circulation and the Foreclosure of Politics," in *Digital Media and Democracy*, edited by Megan Boler (Cambridge, MA: MIT Press, 2008), 101–22.

26   Blood. See also Helmond.

27   For a more detailed account of the concept of the subject supposed to know, see Jodi Dean, *Publicity's Secret: How Technoculture Capitalizes on Democracy:* (Ithaca, NY: Cornell University Press, 2002).

28   Hourihan (see note 23 above).

29   danah boyd, "A Blogger's Blog: Exploring the Definition of a Medium," *reconstruction: studies in contemporary culture* 6.4 (2006). Available at http://reconstruction.eserver.org/064/boyd.shtml (accessed March 23, 2010).

30   For a treatment of blogs as journals, see Asako Miura and Kiyomi Yamashita, "Psychological and Social Influences on Blog Writing: An Online Survey of Blog Authors in Japan," *Journal of Computer-Mediated Communication* 12.4, article 15. Available at http://jcmc.indiana.edu/vol12/issue4/miura.html (accessed March 23, 2010). For a treatment of blogs in terms of journalism, see *Blogging, Citizenship, and the Future of Media*, edited by Mark Tremayne (New York: Routledge, 2007) and Jill Walker Rettberg, *Blogging* (Cambridge, UK: Polity, 2008) chapter 4.

31   The most influential version of blogging as a new form of participatory journalism comes from Dan Gillmor, *We the Media: Grassroots Journalism by the People, for the People* (Cambridge, MA: O'Reilly Media, 2004). For a more nuanced view of bloggers as a "fifth estate" providing checks and balances against the journalistic fourth estate, see Tama Leaver, "The Blogging of Everyday Life," *reconstruction: studies in contemporary culture* 6.4 (2006). Available at http://reconstruction.eserver.org/064/leaver.shtml (accessed March 23, 2010). Leaver extends the

argument from Daniel Drezner and Henry Farrell, "Webs of Influence," *Foreign Policy* (November/December 2004). Available at http://www.foreignpolicy.com/story/cms. php?story_id=2707&popup_delayed=1 (accessed March 23, 2010).

32 For a critical comparison of blogs and newspapers in terms of sourcing, see David Vaina, "Newspapers and Blogs: Closer Than We Think?" *Online Journalism Review* (April 23, 2007). Available at http://www.ojr.org/ojr/stories/070423_vaina/ (accessed March 23, 2010).

33 http://www.blogger.com/tour_pub.g (accessed March 23, 2010).

34 The rest of boyd's approach to blogging is perhaps less convincing. She focuses on three oppositional sets – textuality and orality, corporeality and spatiality, and public and private – which blogging blurs. The oppositional pairs are unconvincing, particularly after the emergence of the printing press. It's difficult to see, then, why framing a discussion of new media in old modernist terms is helpful. Additionally, given her useful complicating of an approach to blogs in terms of singular metaphors and definitions, boyd too quickly resorts to the totalizing image of a blogosphere and of *the* blogosphere as *the* public sphere. There is not a sphere (or world or community) of blogs (just like there is not a sphere or community of paper). There is also not "a" or "the" public. See Dean, *Publicity's Secret*.

35 Cited at http://larvatusprodeo.net/2006/05/09/guy-rundle-on-blogs/ (accessed March 23, 2010).

36 Kaye D. Trammell et al. find that Polish bloggers are motivated primarily by "self-expression"; "Rzeczpospolita blogow [Republic of Blog]: Examining Polish Bloggers Through Content Analysis," *Journal of Computer-Mediated Communication* (2006) 11.3, article 2. Available at http://jcmc.indiana.edu/vol11/issue3/trammell.html (accessed March 23, 2010). The Pew Internet and American Life Project reported in 2006 that 52 percent of American bloggers gave creative self-expression as their major reason for blogging; Amanda Lenhart and Susannah Fox, "Bloggers: A Portrait of the Internet's New Storytellers" (July 19, 2006). Available at http://www.pewinternet.org/~/media/Files/Reports/2006/PIP%20Bloggers%20Report%20July%2019%202006.pdf.pdf (accessed March 23, 2010) . The 2009 State of the Blogosphere reported that "self-expression" continued to be one of the top reasons bloggers blog (October

20, 2009). Available at http://technorati.com/blogging/article/ day-2-the-what-and-why2/ (accessed March 23, 2010).

37 To use Lev Manovich's terms, blogs organize the world as a database rather than through narrative; see *The Language of New Media* (Cambridge, MA: MIT Press, 2001) 225–8.

38 The distinction between orality and literacy comes from Walter Ong, *Orality and Literacy: The Technologizing of the Word* (New York: Routledge, 1982). On second orality, see his unpublished lecture, "Secondary Orality and Secondary Visualism," available at the Walter J. Ong collection, http://libraries.slu.edu/sc/ong/ digital/lectures.html (accessed March 23, 2010). See also Carlo Scannella's posts on Ong at the blog, extensions, http:// cscannella.wordpress.com/2008/04/05/inward-and-outward/ (accessed March 23, 2010). Rettberg also notes the similarity between blogging and oral communication (32–4).

39 Lenhart and Fox's 2006 study for the Pew Internet and American Life Project found that 55 percent of bloggers use a pseudonym.

40 For discussions of the variety of modes of presenting lives and experiences online, see the special issue "Online Lives," edited by John Zuern, *Biography* 26.1 (2003). Available at http://muse.jhu.edu/journals/biography/ (accessed March 23, 2010).

41 Michel Foucault, "Self-Writing," in *Ethics, Subjectivity, and Truth*, edited by Paul Rabinow (New York: The New Press, 1997) 207–22.

42 Foucault 211.

43 Foucault 216.

44 Quoted by John Nicholson, "The Delivery and Confidentiality of Cicero's Letters," *The Classical Journal* 90.1 (Oct.–Nov. 1994) 36.

45 For a thoughtful account of the movement from orality to literacy, see Walter J. Ong, *The Presence of the Word* (New Haven: Yale University Press, 1967).

46 Paul Saenger, *Space between Words: The Origins of Silent Reading* (Stanford, CA: Stanford University Press, 1997).

47 Jocelyn Penny Smith, *Wax Tablets of the Mind* (New York: Routledge, 1997) 240.

48 Thomas N. Habinek, *The Politics of Latin Literature* (Princeton, NJ: Princeton University Press, 1998) 119.

49 Smith 174.

50 Nicholson 33, 63.

51   William A. Johnson, "Toward a Sociology of Reading in Classical Antiquity," *American Journal of Philology* 121 (2000) 620. Habinek emphasizes the diverse variety of writing technologies simultaneously available to the Romans. Choices of medium had social connotations (118–19).

52   Saenger 123.

53   For broader discussions of the role of communications media in imperialism, see Harold Innis, *Empire and Communications* (Lanham, MD: Rowman and Littlefield, 2007) and Armand Mattelart, *Networking the World 1794–2000*, translated by Liz Carey-Libbrecht and James A. Cohen (Minneapolis: University of Minnesota Press, 2000).

54   Slavoj Žižek, *Contingency, Hegemony, Universality*, by Judith Butler, Ernesto Laclau, and Slavoj Žižek (London: Verso, 2000) 117.

55   Žižek, *Contingency* 117.

56   Slavoj Žižek, *Tarrying with the Negative* (Durham, NC: Duke University Press, 1993) 197.

57   Lacan, *Seminar XI* 72.

58   Joan Copjec, *Imagine There's No Woman* (Cambridge, MA: MIT Press, 2002) 213–14.

59   Lacan, *Seminar XI* 104.

60   Slavoj Žižek, *In Defense of Lost Causes* (London: Verso, 2008) 328.

61   From the *Introductory Lectures*, quoted in Jacques Lacan, *The Seminar of Jacques Lacan, Book VII: The Ethics of Psychoanalysis*, edited by Jacques-Alain Miller, translated by Dennis Porter (New York: W.W. Norton, 1992) 71.

62   Lacan, *Seminar XI* 177.

63   Copjec 43.

64   Copjec 53.

65   Lacan, *Seminar XI* 169.

Chapter 3   Whatever Blogging

1   The Pew Internet and American Life Project reported on July 19, 2006 that the majority of US bloggers (54 percent) are under thirty; Amanda Lenhart and Susanna Fox, "Bloggers: A Portrait of the Internet's New Storytellers," available at http://www.pewinternet.org/pdfs/PIP%20Bloggers%20Report%20

July%2019%202006.pdf (accessed March 23, 2010). Pew reported on December 19, 2007 that "girls dominate the teen blogosphere; 35% of all online teen girls blog, compared with 20% of online teen boys"; Amanda Lenhart, Mary Madden, Aaron Smith, and Alexandra Macgill, "Teens and Social Media," available at http://www.pewinternet.org/Reports/2007/Teens-and-Social-Media.aspx (accessed March 25, 2010).

2   Lenhart and Fox.

3   See Chuck Salter, "Girl Power," posted December 19, 2007. Available at http://www.fastcompany.com/magazine/118/girl-power.html?page=0%2C0 (accessed March 25, 2010). See also http://www.whateverlife.com.

4   http://www.whateverradio.com/website/shop.php.

5   "State of the Blogosphere 2008." Available at http://technorati.com/blogging/state-of-the-blogosphere/ (accessed March 25, 2010).

6   See also James Grimmelmann, "Saving Facebook," *Iowa Law Review* 94 (2009) 1137–1206. Available at http://works.bepress.com/james_grimmelmann/20/ (accessed March 25, 2010).

7   Dominic Pettman, *Love and Other Technologies* (New York: Fordham University Press, 2006) 9.

8   Giorgio Agamben, *The Coming Community*, translated by Michael Hardt (Minneapolis: University of Minnesota Press, 1993) 1.

9   Herman Melville, "Bartleby the Scrivener," was first published in *Putnam's Monthly Magazine* in 1853.

10   Susan Buck-Morss, *Dreamworld and Catastrophe* (Cambridge, MA: MIT Press, 2000) 140.

11   Buck-Morss 147.

12   One significant study of film as a vehicle for assimilation is Michael Rogin, *Blackface, White Noise* (Berkeley: University of California Press, 1998).

13   Buck-Morss 161.

14   Buck-Morss 159.

15   Buck-Morss 201.

16   Buck-Morss 201.

17   Buck-Morss 147.

18   Mark C. Taylor, *Confidence Games: Money and Markets in a World without Redemption* (Chicago: University of Chicago Press, 2004) 294.

19   Michael Hardt and Antonio Negri, *Empire* (Cambridge, MA: Harvard University Press, 2000) 197.

20 Zygmunt Bauman, *Liquid Love* (Cambridge, UK: Polity, 2003) 50–1.

21 Hardt and Negri 214.

22 Hardt and Negri 216.

23 Cayley Sorochan, "Flash Mobs and Urban Gaming: Networked Performances in Urban Space," Master's Thesis, Department of Art History and Communication Studies, McGill University, Montreal.

24 Agamben 47–8.

25 Agamben 63.

26 Jean Baudrillard, *In the Shadow of Silent Majorities*, translated by Paul Foss, John Johnston, Paul Patton, and Andrew Berardini (Los Angeles, CA: Semiotext(e), 2007) 38.

27 Baudrillard 61.

28 Agamben 65.

29 Agamben 85.

30 Agamben 6.

31 Agamben 85.

32 Agamben 87.

33 Baudrillard 56

34 Guy Debord, *The Society of the Spectacle*, translated by Donald Nicholson-Smith (New York: Zone Books, 1999) 133.

35 Debord 136.

36 Agamben 80.

37 Agamben 83.

38 Sigmund Freud, "Instincts and their Vicissitudes," *The Standard Edition of the Complete Psychological Works of Sigmund Freud, Volume XIV (1914–1916): On the History of the Psycho-Analytic Movement, Papers on Metapsychology and Other Works*, edited by James Strachey (London: Hogarth Press, 1915) 109–40; 127.

39 Jacques Lacan, *The Seminar of Jacques Lacan, Book XI: The Four Fundamental Concepts of Psychoanalysis*, edited by Jacques-Alain Miller, translated by Alan Sheridan (New York: W.W. Norton, 1981) 185.

40 Agamben 65.

41 Jacques Lacan, *The Seminar of Jacques Lacan, Book XVII: The Other Side of Psychoanalysis*, edited by Jacques-Alain Miller, translated by Russell Grigg (New York: W.W. Norton, 2007).

42 Slavoj Žižek, *Iraq: The Borrowed Kettle* (London: Verso, 2004) 144.

43 Lacan, *Seminar XVII*, 107.

Chapter 4   Affective Networks

1   Jacques Lacan, *The Seminar of Jacques Lacan, Book XVII: The Other Side of Psychoanalysis*, edited by Jacques-Alain Miller, translated by Russell Grigg (New York: W.W. Norton, 2007) 147.

2   Slavoj Žižek, *Tarrying with the Negative* (Durham, NC: Duke University Press, 1993) 203–6.

3   Friedrich A. Kittler, *Gramophone, Film, Typewriter*, translated by Geoffrey Winthrop-Young and Michael Wutz (Stanford, CA: Stanford University Press, 1999) 1.

4   Kittler 2.

5   Eric Lipton, Eric Schmitt, and Mark Mazzetti, "Review of Jet Bomb Plot Shows More Missed Clues," *New York Times* (January 17, 2010). Available at http://www.nytimes.com/2010/01/18/us/18intel.html?pagewanted=1&hp (accessed March 26, 1010).

6   "Technical Flaws Hinder Terrorist Watch List; Congress Calls for Investigation," House Committee on Science and Technology press release issued August 21, 2008. Available at http://science.house.gov/Press/PRArticle.aspx?NewsID=2289 (accessed March 26, 2010).

7   Kittler 258.

8   Slavoj Žižek, *The Parallax View* (Cambridge, MA: MIT University Press, 2006) 63.

9   Alexander Zaitchik, "Twitter Nation Has Arrived: How Scared Should We Be?," *Alternet*, posted February 21, 2009. Available at http://www.alternet.org/media/127623?page=3 (accessed March 26, 2010).

10   Clive Thompson, "How Twitter Creates a Social Sixth Sense," *Wired* 15.07, posted June 26, 2007. Available at http://www.wired.com/techbiz/media/magazine/15-07/st_thompson (accessed March 26, 2010).

11   Lauren Berlant, "Faceless book," Supervalent Thought, posted December 25, 2007. Available at http://supervalentthought.com/2007/12/25/faceless-book/ (accessed March 26, 2010).

12   Alex Cheng and Mark Evans, "Inside Twitter," Sysomos Inc., posted June 2009. Available at http://sysomos.com/insidetwitter/ (accessed March 26, 2010).

13   Peter Cashmore, "Twitter Zombies: 24% of Tweets Created by Bots," posted August 6, 2009. Available at http://mashable.com/2009/08/06/twitter-bots/ (accessed March 26, 2010). See

also Clay Shirky, "Power Laws, Weblogs, and Inequality" (February 8, 2003). Available at http://www.shirky.com/writings/powerlaw_weblog.html. Cheng and Evans 2.

14 Cheng and Evans 25.

15 David Barstow, "Behind TV Analysts, Pentagon's Hidden Hand," *New York Times* (April 20, 2008). Available at http://www.nytimes.com/2008/04/20/us/20generals. html?pagewanted=all (accessed March 26, 2010).

16 Barstow.

17 Tiziana Terranova, *Network Culture: Politics for the Information Age* (New York: Pluto Press, 2005) 14.

18 For a more detailed discussion of the shift from messages to contributions, see my *Democracy and Other Neoliberal Fantasies* (Durham, NC: Duke University Press, 2009) chapter 1.

19 See also my critique of Mark Hansen's account of perception: Jodi Dean, "The Real Internet," *International Journal of Žižek Studies* 4.1 (2010). Available at http://zizekstudies.org/index. php/ijzs/issue/archive (accessed March 26, 2010).

20 Terranova 25.

21 The quoted passage is from Terranova 142.

22 Robert J. Shiller, *Irrational Exuberance* (Princeton, NJ: Princeton University Press, 2000) 21. The text of Greenspan's speech is available at http://www.federalreserve.gov/boarddocs/ speeches/1996/19961205.htm (accessed March 26, 2010).

23 On pushing the internet into the private sector, see M. Mitchell Waldrop, *The Dream Machine: J.C.R. Licklider and the Revolution that Made Computing Personal* (New York: Viking, 2001) 464.

24 John Cassidy, *dot.con* (New York: HarperCollins, 2002) 267.

25 Kevin Kelly, *New Rules for the Economy* (New York: Penguin, 1998), 153.

26 Shiller 151–3. Information cascades designate the same phenomenon Barabási describes in terms of power law distributions in networks characterized by growth, choice, and preferential attachment; see Albert-László Barabási, *Linked* (New York: Plume, 2003).

27 Cassidy 250.

28 Cassidy 229.

29 Cassidy 225.

30 Kelly 159.

31 Justin Fox, *The Myth of the Rational Market* (New York: HarperCollins, 2009) 238.

32   Chris Anderson, "The End of Theory: The Data Deluge Makes the Scientific Method Obsolete," *Wired* 16.07, posted June 23, 2008. Available at http://www.wired.com/science/discoveries/magazine/16-07/pb_theory (accessed March 26, 2010). Critical responses can be found at *Edge*: http://www.edge.org/discourse/the_end_of_theory.html (accessed March 26, 2010).

33   Guy Debord, *Comments on the Society of the Spectacle*, translated by Malcolm Imrie (London: Verso, 1998) 9.

34   Debord 27 (emphasis added).

35   Debord 29.

36   Debord 22.

37   Debord 19.

38   Debord 17.

39   Debord 18.

40   Mark Andrejevic, *iSpy: Surveillance and Power in the Interactive Era* (Lawrence: University Press of Kansas, 2007) 160.

41   Debord 11–12.

42   Debord 15.

43   From her introduction to *The Affective Turn*, edited by Patricia Ticineto Clough with Jean Halley (Durham, NC: Duke University Press, 2007) 1–33; 3.

44   Michael Hardt and Antonio Negri, *Empire* (Cambridge, MA: Harvard University Press, 2000) 293.

45   Alexander R. Galloway and Eugene Thacker, *The Exploit* (Minneapolis: University of Minnesota Press, 2007) 155.

46   Terranova 51.

47   Terranova 42.

48   Joan Copjec, "May '68, the Emotional Month," in *Lacan: The Silent Partners*, edited by Slavoj Žižek (London: Verso, 2006) 90–114; 95.

49   Copjec 102.

50   Copjec follows Lacan in attributing the change to the shift from the discourse of the master to the discourse of the university, itself a capitalist formation. Rather than following this temporalization, I view both elements as aspects of contemporary society.

51   Copjec 105.

52   The Talking Heads' song "Once in a Lifetime," from the 1980 album *Remain in Light*, is perhaps the best pop treatment of anxiety as a suffocating confrontation with enjoyment's relation to the unbearable openness of the past not lived. (Recorded by Talking Heads, written by Brian Eno, Jerry Harrison, David Byrne, Tina Weymouth, and Chris Franz. Lyrics available at

http://www.lyricsfreak.com/t/talking+heads/once+in+a+lifetime_20135070.html. Accessed March 26, 2010.)

53   Žižek, *Tarrying*, 206.
54   Copjec 109.
55   Lacan 105–6.
56   Žižek, *Parallax* 61.
57   See Ned Rossiter, *Organized Networks: Media Theory, Creative Labour, New Institutions* (Rotterdam: NAi Publishers, 2006).
58   Paulo Virno has already raised a similar point in his critique of Marx's "fragment on machines." Virno writes:
For example, at the end of the "Fragment" Marx claims that in a communist society, rather than an amputated worker, the whole individual will produce. That is the individual who has changed as a result of a large amount of free time, cultural consumption and a sort of "power to enjoy". Most of us will recognise that the Postfordist labouring process actually takes advantage in its way of this very transformation albeit depriving it of all emancipatory qualities. What is learned, carried out and consumed in the time outside of labour is then utilised in the production of commodities, becomes a part of the use value of labour power and is computed as profitable resource. Even the greater "power to enjoy" is always on the verge of being turned into a labouring task. ("General Intellect," translated by Arianna Bove. Available at http://www.generation-online.org/p/fpvirno10.htm [accessed March 22, 2010])
59   Žižek, *Parallax* 26.
60   Žižek, *Parallax* 26.
61   Andrejevic documents the cycle of suspicion with respect to forms of peer-to-peer monitoring and surveillance.
62   Thomas Elsaesser, "'Constructive Instability,' or the Life of Things as Cinema's Afterlife?," in *Video Vortex: Reader Responses to YouTube*, edited by Geert Lovink and Sabine Niederer (Amsterdam: Institute for Network Cultures, 2008) 13–31; 30.
63   Christian Marazzi, *Capital and Language*, translated by Gregory Conti (Los Angeles, CA: Semiotext(e), 2008) 23. He writes, "The *mimetic relationship* between the individual economic actor and the others (the aggressive 'crowd' of investors/speculators) has its rationality in everyone's lack of knowledge' (129).
64   See Sophie Statzel's excellent "Cybersupremacy: The New Face and Form of White Supremacist Activism," *Digital Media and Democracy*, edited by Megan Boler (Cambridge, MA: MIT Press, 2008) 405–28.

Index